Beginners Guide to Critical Thinking and Problem Solving

Become a Better Critical Thinker & Problem Solver, by Using Secret Tools & Techniques That Will Boost These Skills & Your Decision Making Now!

By Pamela Hughes

Table of Content

Chapter 1: How To Develop Skills In Critical Thinking

What is Critical Thinking?
Skills in Critical Thinking
Facts and Logic
Intellectual Rigor
Seeking Straight Answers
Thinking About Your Thought
You're The One In Charge
Brainstorming for Critical Thinking
Rules of Brainstorming
The Process of Brainstorming
Bloom's Taxonomy and Critical Thinking

Chapter 2: Framework and Tools for Critical Thinking

Step-by-Step Critical Thinking for Problem Solving
The Framework of Critical Thinking
Tools for Critical Thinking/Intellectual standards
Intellectual Traits

Chapter 3: Benefits of Critical Thinking

Qualities of a Good Critical Thinker
When to Apply Critical Thinking
To Improve Something
Specific Daily Activities Where Critical Thinking Can Be Used
When to Use Critical Thinking

Chapter 4: Routines to Improve Critical Thinking

Taking Deep Breaths
Be A Keen Reader And A Sound Synthesizer Information
Practice Self-talk
Practice Goal Setting
Know Your Weaknesses

Travel Widely
Best Practices for Improving Critical Thinking Skills

Chapter 5: Techniques, Strategies, And Skills

Strategies for Developing Critical Thinking in Students
How To Teach Critical Thinking In Schools
Teaching Strategies For Critical Thinking Skills

Chapter 6: Types of Critical Thinking

Logical Reasoning
Scientific Reasoning
The Psychology of Critical Thinking
Theoretical Domain
Methodology Domain
Practical Domain

Chapter 7: Exercise For Critical Thinking

Time To Think Critically
Analysis Facts And Applying Logic
Critical Thinking Exercise
Critical Thinking For Students
Critical Thinking in the Workplace
Powerful Skills Related To Critical Thinking

Chapter 8: Critical Thinking Vs Non-Critical Thinking

What is Non-Critical Thinking?
When Do Non-Critical Thinking Likely To Happen To You?
Background of Critical Thinking
Differences between Critical Thinking and Ordinary
Thinking
Characteristics of Critical Thinkers
Eating Habits that Boost your Critical Thinking
Obstacles of Critical Thinking and How to Overcome Them

Critical Habits of the Mind

Chapter 9: Problem-Solving—Steps, Process, and Techniques

    Definition Of A Problem
    Problem Analysis
    Synthesis Of A Problem
    Importance of Problem Solving
    The Problem Solving Process
    Techniques and tools needed for Problem Solving
    Barriers of Problem Solving

Chapter 10: Problem Solving Skills

Introduction

Congratulations on purchasing *BEGINNERS GUIDE TO CRITICAL THINKING AND PROBLEM SOLVING: Become a Better Critical Thinker & Problem Solver, by Using Secret Tools & Techniques That Will Boost These Skills & Your Decision Making Now!* and thank you for doing so. Whether or not we think creatively and critically can determine the success and failures in every aspect of our lives. The human brain is always prone to distortions, irrationality, cognitive biases, and prejudices, which in most cases affect our ability to reason. By purchasing this book, you have taken the first step towards learning how to become a better person in communication through effective critical thinking and problem solving skills. The information that you find in the following chapters is very important as it will help you to take control of every situation you are in due to the ability to consider multiple world views.

To that end, this book provides an in-depth overview of critical thinking, highlighting its framework and elements, as well as its day-to-day use. It covers the universal intellectual traits of a critical thinker, including courage, humility, empathy, autonomy, integrity, perseverance and confidence. The book will comprehensively address the key strategies that are necessary in developing critical thinking skills. An interesting concept covered in this book is the qualities of a good critical thinker, which can help you measure your critical thinking skills. With this knowledge, you will be able to learn how to become a quality problem solver and one who can think of problems in different perspectives.

There are several books tackling the significance of critical thinking in the market, thanks again for choosing this one! I ensured that the book is full of as much useful information as possible. Please enjoy reading!

Chapter 1: How To Develop Skills In Critical Thinking

Times are changing, and whether we like it or not, the way we live and work has changed over time, thanks to globalization and technological innovations. First, we are increasingly facing complex problems, which affect the society including economic depression, global warming, financial crises, and pollution. Faced with diverse options for problem solving, we are forced to develop good thinking and generate creative ideas in an effort to solve the problems. On the other hand, globalization and technology have both affected our personal lives. We have excess information available around us, and what we learn on a daily basis may become obsolete in the near future. Amidst the benefits of information, we increasingly face even more challenges as we compete with talented people across the world. In order to be successful, we must possess good thinking skills for reliable decision-making and proper reasoning.

But what does it mean to have good thinking skills? Having good thinking skills means that you avoid the 2 major flaws of reasoning: having sense of absurdity and sense of obviousness. It means that you become a critical thinker, a person adept with skills that can enable him/her steer through complexities of the world. Good thinking skills can enable us to achieve the intellectual integrity needed to make sound decisions.

Therefore, in this chapter, we are going to have a clear understanding of the concept of critical thinking, who a critical thinker is, and the skills that a critical thinker possesses.

What is Critical Thinking?

Critical thinking refers to one's ability to think rationally and clearly, understanding the connection between logical ideas. The concept has been a subject of much debate since the times of Greek philosophers such as Socrates and Plato, and has continued to be an important discussion subject in the modern era. Critical thinking might be described as one's ability to engage in independent and reflective thinking before making a decision. It is about being an active learner instead of a passive information recipient.

Critical thinkers ask rigorous questions about ideas and assumptions rather than just believing in every information they get in at the face value. Critical thinkers will always attempt to know whether arguments, ideas, or findings represent the true picture and are very open to finding out if they are not.

When you think critically, you get to constantly challenge the information you are given. Say, in the classroom, even if a mathematical formula seems obvious and statistically prove, you will still try to identify a new and better formula.

The basic concept of critical thinking is very simple: it is an art of taking charge of your own mind. Its value is similarly simple: if you can take charge of your mind, you can equally take charge of your life, which mean improving yourself, bringing your mind under self-control. Critical thinking means being interested in how the mind works, how to modify and fine-tune the mind, and how to monitor it for better functioning. It involves engaging yourself in the habit of questioning every aspect of your life.

Skills in Critical Thinking

Although there is no universal standard to the specific skills needed to be an excellent critical thinker, there are 6 key skills that will help you. Focusing on these can help you develop exceptional critical thinking capability.

1. Identification

In order to be exceptional in critical thinking, the first thing to do is to identify the problem or situation as well as the internal and external factors that may be surrounding it. Once you understand the situation and the factors, groups, or people surrounding it, you can begin to think deeper into the issue and start brainstorming the possible solutions.

When thinking of a problem, it is important to ask yourself the following questions:

- What is the problem?
- Who is doing what?
- What reasons explain the situation?
- What are the effects, and could these change?

2. Research

When making a decision about an issue or comparing the arguments for and against the issue, the ability to perform independent research is key. Every argument should be persuasive. Most facts and figures supporting a particular argument may be lacking context or coming from questionable sources. This can be addressed by performing an independent verification, finding sources of information, and evaluating the most reliable.

3. Identifying biases

The skill of identifying biases in an argument can be very difficult since even the smartest people fail to recognize biases. An effective critical thinker is able to evaluate information objectively and judge both sides of the argument. As you evaluate claims, it is important to understand that there are possible biases posed by each side of the argument.

Equally, it is important to learn how to keep away from personal biases when assessing a particular situation. Put yourself in a situation where you are able to equally evaluate the claims of both sides of an argument, and make an effective judgment.

While evaluating an argument, it is important to consider the following questions:
- Who is going to benefit from this school of thought?
- Does the source of information have an agenda?
- Is the information source leaving out information that does not support its claims?
- Does the source use unnecessary language to sway the perception of the audience?

4. Inference
Another important critical thinking skill is the ability to infer and draw conclusions based on the information that you are presented with. Information does not come with its meaning spelled out easily. Therefore, you need to assess it and draw conclusions based on the raw data.

Being able to infer a conclusion means that you can discover and extrapolate potential outcomes of a situation. However, keep in mind that not all inferences are accurate; some data may alter the conclusion of an argument.

5. Determining relevance
A key challenging aspect of critical thinking is figuring out what information is important for one to consider. In many instances, you will be presented with information that may appear important, but they may turn out to be very minute data points to consider in making a decision.

6. Curiosity
It is very easy to take every argument presented to you at face value. However, this can be dangerous when you are faced with

situations that need critical thinking. As people get older, they easily get acquainted with the habit of refraining from asking questions, but this is not an effective approach for a critical thinker. Being able to ask open-ended questions is the best way to learn and gain knowledge if you are a critical thinker.

Facts and Logic

Critical thinking process entails evaluating which arguments have logic and are factual with the aim of separating the truth from falsehood. Both facts and logics are essential elements for making good judgment.

Facts

The internet makes 'fact-checking' any report inconceivably snappy and straightforward- although there are a ton of wonky sites and you may aggravate an error if you favor a website page to a painstakingly researched book. In any case, however, you have to search for a few kinds of proof in literary work, of which 'facts' are the most superficial layer. Uncritical readers, as a rule, think that evidence is about facts- yet critical readers go significantly further. They do not read primarily to find acts; like great logicians, they realize that the 'fact of the matter' is not basic and that any number of potential facts exist. Instead, they expect to fundamentally assess thoughts and arguments, mindful that the significant decisions come in the creator's selection and arrangement of the facts.

Weighing up primary and secondary sources for facts

Primary sources are a critical thinker's gold dust. They are unique materials from the timeline included that have not been sifted through translation or evaluation. Primary sources present different reasoning, present and report discoveries, or offer new thoughts or data. Secondary sources are bits of news coverage, or a book about another person's opinions, research or works. They are translations and assessments written in retrospection.

Consider the *Global Warming* discussion and precisely number of facts exist on the two sides in the debate. If you look at various sites, arguing over the very same bit of news (that the Greenland ice sheet has been accounted for as shrinking), you can discover two definitive and similarly factual explanations that reach contradictory conclusions. Keep in mind in this discussion, as in many others, the facts selection is what is important. That is why it is essential to look 'behind the facts' as well.

When reading a primary source, a short statement gives you a gold-plated proof for your argument- while being all the more impressive. For instance, if you are trusting that a researcher will demonstrate to you that a paper called the Daily Wail once cautioned that polar bears were in threat of extinction, then a statement from the writing itself is better than anything else. The Daily Wail would be, for this situation, the primary source. However, to accept the same article as evidence that specialists take that polar bears are dying (not to mention that they are) is using the paper as a secondary source.

The issue with secondary sources is that the meaning might be distinctive in the first context. If you are going through someone's views on another person's perspectives, which is the thing that practically all composing comes down to, consider the creator being the channel; as opposed to believing the person in question to have precisely passed on any other person's words. Hence, select the content that you use cautiously-critically. The more drawn out the chain of sources, the more probable contortions are to show up (as in a round of Chinese Whispers).

Logic

Logic refers to the science of how people evaluate reasoning and arguments. It is not about opinions, but how arguments should be formed to ensure they are correct and reasonable. As such, a logical argument is that which has sufficiently justified premises that are appropriately relevant to the conclusion. In order to remain logical, an argument should consider the following:

Logical form— understanding the form of an argument is important to make good deductive reasoning. For instance, by stating that, "if Plato is a man, then he is immortal," then the logical form, "if A, then B," makes a good argumentation.

Logical validity—Logical arguments have premises that guarantee the right conclusion. An invalid argument does not give us any reason to believe in the truth of the conclusion. In such a case, the premises could be true, and the conclusion becomes false.

Argument interpretation—It is also important that critical thinkers understand people's arguments and be able to clarify them. One should be able to distinguish between the premises and the conclusion. Sometimes it is also necessary to identify assumptions and creativity in order to understand a logical argument.

Some of the questions that can help you make your arguments logical include:
- Do all the arguments or statements you make logically fit together?
- Does the argument make sense?
- Does the argument flow in line with the current situation?

Intellectual Rigor

One of the fundamental elements of critical thinking is intellectual rigor. This refers to clarity among critical thinkers and their ability to think deeply and carefully with rigor when facing challenging arguments or new knowledge. Having this potential means that one can engage in a constructive argument and methodologically explore ideas, philosophies, and theories.

In critical thinking, the intellectual rigor of a statement is essential. If the statement or problem to be addressed is put in an unclear way, it will be hard to understand it. If unclear statements are used to make decisions, the result is always uncertain. The language used here should be easily understood by the parties involved. Take care of the language and beliefs of the participants to avoid using terms that may bring out contradicting meanings.

You might be wondering how to differentiate between a clear (rigor) and unclear statement. Here is an example to help you understand the difference.

What needs to be done on the food shortage issue?

The above question lacks intellectual rigor and is somehow tricky to address since one is not aware of what the person asking the question considers to be the problem. Clarity here would be achieved by pointing out the main issue of concern and rephrasing the question to:

What does the government need to do to ensure that its citizens have enough food supply and that there is no drought and famine in the country?

The second question is easily understood, making it simple to analyze the causes of drought and famine and possible measures to counter it. A clear problem statement makes the critical thinking process effective. Be sure to make your statement, thoughts, and arguments clear.

To achieve intellectual rigor, you can ask the following questions:

- Can you give an example?
- Can you express the statement differently?
- Can you further elaborate on that point?

Seeking Straight Answers

It is tempting to imagine that critical thinkers are always interested in complex answers which they have to comprehensively examine in order to get the message. However, this is not the case. Critical thinkers prefer straight answers that will aid them to determine the reasoning behind an argument, the meaning of the premises, and how the conclusion is derived from the arguments.

In order to get straight answers, critical thinking requires that you ask the right questions. To enhance the questioning process when addressing an issue, it is recommended that you break down the questions.

Suppose you encountered a certain problem, at school or at work, and you are not sure how to go about it. In order to get straight answers to the situation, ask yourself the following questions:

- What information about this situation do I have already?
- How do I know the above information?
- What is my goal in trying to discover, prove/disapprove, or support?
- What would I be overlooking?

These questions encourage you to have right, straight answers to a problem. If it helps, try to write down the answers to the above questions when faced with a problem. The same strategy can also be used to coax others towards getting specific answers.

Thinking About Your Thought

Most people who assume that they are the best critical thinkers always forget about themselves, always arrogantly critiquing other people's reasoning and thoughts. However, a good critical thinker is one who engages more in self-reflection, always trying to think more about their thoughts.

It is important that you keep your eye on your own thoughts. Think of where the thoughts began, how they look like, and where they are leading you. The human brain is always impressive and can sort information accurately, but lack of self-reflection can encourage us to ignore important thoughts.

The brain has the tendency of using heuristics to make quick inferences about situations we are facing. In many instances, such heuristics can yield reliable results and help us solve problems. However, in other cases, they form unreliable biases that direct us to the wrong path.

You're The One In Charge

A critical thinker must remain alert at all times. In order to be in charge of your thoughts and make accurate judgments of situations, it is important to utilize analytical skills.

It is easy for you to accept arguments made, especially in public to be true. It is also natural to think that you are being told the truth about claims, and you end up accepting them at face value. However, you should not blindly accept what you are told or what read. Don't assume that because something has been asserted in spoken or printed form, then it is entirely accurate, and you must agree with it.

Being in charge means that you should be aware that people make false assertions for several reasons, such as to deceive you into altering your opinion about someone or something. Some false statements are also made out of carelessness or ignorance. Other claims, though may bear some truth, are greatly exaggerated while others are oversimplified or are just rough guesses.

This means then you should always avoid accepting claims or arguments at face value. Learn to keep an open and analytical mind. However, it might be difficult for you always to determine whether a claim is true or false; the best method you can use in deciding whether the claim is justified is the evaluation method. A claim that lacks enough evidence to support it is unwarranted. So, in essence, a claim is justified if it is accurate and unjustified if it is not. However, a claim can be true but unreasonable if the person making it does not provide a good ground for believing it.

When making judgments, always remember that the standard of claims is such that it is either true or false. There are no claims that are half true or half false or in between. True means the whole truth and doesn't allow approximations or degrees.

As a critical thinker, when you want to be in charge of every judgment, you need to qualify an argument by stating the standards that you are applying. Use expressions like:
- Completely justified
- Entirely justified
- Wholly justified

Always choose the right qualifications for the judgments you make about claims and their justifications

Brainstorming for Critical Thinking

Brainstorming is a popular problem solving technique used by critical thinkers because of the freedom it creates in all directions in search of the most effective solutions. The main aim of brainstorming is always to create an arsenal of alternative solutions. Brainstorming is not simply a means to some end. It is more than that as it involves developing a creative and critical mind and heightening curiosity. With curiosity, our minds open up to see diverse perspectives of a particular viewpoint, which in turn enhances problem solving.

Rules of Brainstorming

The brainstorming process may seem not to have any constraints, but the success depends on the consideration of the rules below.

Pick a time and place—The brainstorming, our brains always function at the greatest capacity. It is important to time when everyone is in good spirits and rested because students need the energy to advance their thinking potential.

Encourage wild ideas and discussions— It is important to assign someone to be in charge of writing down the ideas discussed in order to keep the group focused. You need to choose someone who can write down legibly and quickly.

Go for quantity—Take your time to use the tools needed for brainstorming to generate a long list of potential options. By generating many ideas, you are able to analyze and identify the best solution.

Set a time limit—When you focus on generating ideas, you will be exhilarated because the process of brainstorming requires maximum brain capacity. Thus, you should ensure that brainstorming does not take more than an hour.

Write down and organize all the ideas— Ensure that everyone can see the ideas shared and written down. Organize the ideas into different categories. For instance, you could organize the reasons to "why it is wrong to steal" under the following categories:

- **Moral reason**: "Because every religion is against it."
- **Practical reason**: "It disorganizes the society."
- **Odd reason**: "If I took someone's item when they are not around, use it and return before they notice, would that be stealing?"

Get rid of bad ideas—Review the list of ideas and cull the bad ones, until you remain with the best. While brainstorming, most of the ideas will be useless. Once you are done brainstorming, spend time to discuss which of the ideas are actually the best.

The Process of Brainstorming

Brainstorming can involve one person or a group of people. Involving multiple people in the process can help in achieving consensus more so if the ideas being proposed require a significant change or solution.

Regardless of the number of people involved in brainstorming, the most effective process is outlined below:

1. Define the problem
Before you begin brainstorming, you need to clearly identify the problem you are trying to address. You should be able to identify the specific goals and objectives meant to solve the

problem as well as the causes and effects. If, for example, you continuously fail in a subject, your objective to solve it should be, "to increase the time I spend in the library studying the subject," or "to begin attending extra tuition on the subject." The objective can help you think of the problem and solution in a more abstract manner.

2. Collect your tools

The main aim of brainstorming is to get ideas out of your mind and put them into a book as fast as possible. Apart from writing down, you many use mind maps and brainwriting (in case of group brainstorming) to help in organizing your thoughts. Begin noting down all the ideas you have about the problem. It is important note that there are no bad ideas

3. Focus your ideas

Once you have prepared the brainstorming tools, you need to begin jotting down the ideas you think about as quickly as possible. Delve into the ideas, which you think are the strongest and can be implemented to address the problem. Keep in mind that there are no bad ideas; think of many solutions as much as you can to obtain a better solution.

4. Narrow down the list of ideas

After making a mind map or a list of ideas, focus on narrowing down the number of ideas to 2 or 3. In order to ensure that the ones you choose are the best, ask yourself the following questions:

- Am I able to implement this idea with the existing resources I have?
- Has the idea I have chosen been implemented before? And what was the end result?
- Who do I need to convince about the idea?
- Does this idea need a behavioral or cultural change?
- Is this the right time for the chosen idea?

4. Define and act on the best solution

After narrowing down the list of ideas to top 2 or 3 ideas, you will now need to further analyze the best solution from the alternative. Check the solution that can easily be implemented then plan for action.

Bloom's Taxonomy and Critical Thinking

Bloom's taxonomy is a set of hierarchical models used to classify educational learning objectives, levels of complexity and specificity. It is the hierarchical ordering of cognitive skills that can help in teaching and learning. Bloom's taxonomy is applicable in vast areas of knowledge including critical thinking.

Lower Order Thinking Skills

Lower order thinking is the foundation of skills required to move into higher-order thinking. These skills are taught well in school systems and include activities such as reading and writing. In lower-order thinking, the information does not need to be applied to any real-life examples. It only needs to be understood and recalled.

Higher-Order Thinking Skills

Higher-order thinking skills distinguish critical thinking from lower-order learning outcomes such as those attuned by rote memorizations. Higher-order thinking skills includes synthesizing, analyzing, reasoning, comprehending, application and evaluation. HOTS is based on various taxonomies of learning especially the one created by Benjamin Bloom which lays a lot of emphasis on analysis, synthesis, and evaluation.

Bloom's taxonomy is designed with six levels to promote higher-order thinking. The HOTS requires understanding and applying the knowledge learned from lower-order thinking skills.

The top three levels of Bloom's taxonomy displayed in a pyramid are analysis, synthesis, and evaluation. These levels of taxonomy all involve critical or higher-order thinking. Students who can think are those who can apply the knowledge and skills they have learned to new concepts.

Bloom and Critical Thinking Models

Bloom's taxonomy describes the significant areas in the cognitive domain. The following are the essential models of thinking according to Bloom

Knowledge

The taxonomy begins by defining knowledge the ability to remember previously learned material, knowledge according to Bloom represents the lowest level of learning outcomes in the cognitive domain

Comprehension

Knowledge is then followed by comprehension or the ability to grasp the meaning of the material. This goes beyond the knowledge level. Comprehension is the lowest level of understanding.

Application

This is the next area in the hierarchy. It refers to the ability to use learned material in new and concrete principles and theories. The application requires a higher level of understanding than comprehension

Analysis

This is the next level of taxonomy in which the learning outcomes requires an understanding of both the content and the structural form of the material

Synthesis
The next level of taxonomy refers to the ability to put parts together to form a new whole. Learning outcomes at this level stress the creative behaviors with a significant emphasis on the formulation of new patterns or structures. You move beyond relying on previously learned information or analyzing the material, and you attempt to put the parts or information you have reviewed together to create new meaning or new structure.

Evaluation
This is the last level of the taxonomy. It concerns the ability to judge the value of the material for a given purpose. Learning outcomes in this area are the highest in the cognitive hierarchy because they incorporate or contain elements of knowledge, comprehension, application, analysis, and synthesis. They also provide conscious value judgment based on a defined criterion.

Chapter 2: Framework and Tools for Critical Thinking

In every single act that we engage in or any decision that we make in our day-to-day lives, thinking is mandatory. Starting from what to eat, what to wear, how to handle school work and work projects as well the investment decisions to make, all require the active involvement of your mind. Some of the decisions you make are complex in nature and require smart thinking, which in this case, you have to think critically. Decisions that need critical thinking are known to have lasting effects on your life, work, or business. For example, a business investment decision will call for smart thinking since your finances, and the life of your investment may be adversely affected by poor decision-making. Other choices, which are minor such as what to eat or what to wear, do not necessarily call for critical thinking.

To undertake critical thinking effectively, you need to understand the framework and tools for critical thinking. Scholars and researchers have worked continually over the years to come up with the standard framework and tools for critical thinking. Continue reading through this chapter to understand the basics of the universally accepted standards of critical thinking.

Step-by-Step Critical Thinking for Problem Solving

A critical thinking process helps our minds to focus, rather than jumping into conclusions. It guides our minds through reasonable steps that widen our perspectives, consider possibilities, and put side biases when making judgments. The process of critical thinking involves 6 steps discussed below:

1. Knowledge

When addressing a problem, clear vision helps us to be on the right track. This first step in critical thinking identifies the problem or argument that needs to be addressed. It is necessary to ask questions in order to have a deep understanding of the problem. The questions at this stage should to open-ended in order to explore and discuss the problem critically. The 2 main questions to answer in this stage are:

- What is the situation?
- Why do I need to address the problem?

2. Comprehension

In the second step, the problem is reviewed further to understand the facts aligning it and the situation. Data is collected regarding the problem through the use of research method. The methodology chosen depends on the problem to be addressed, the deadline to solve it, and the type of data that is available.

3. Application

This step involves the continued assessment of the problem by understanding the different resources and facts used to solve the problem. The information and resources used to tackle the problem are linked to determine the best way to address the problem. Mind maps may be used in this stage to analyze the situation.

4. Analysis

After the information has been collected and linked to the main problem, a critical thinker analyses the situation to identify both the strong points and weak points of the situation as well as challenges faced during the implementation of the solution. At this stage, the priorities are set to determine how the problem is to be solved. One of the common techniques that can be used to analyze the problem is the cause–effect diagram; this is usually used to categorize the causes of the problem and the impact.

5. Synthesis

After problem analysis, one should relate all the collected information and form a decision about solving the problem. The critical thinker identifies the routes to follow in order to implement the action. If there are more than one solutions, they should be evaluated to find the most advantageous solution. A common tool used to synthesis the problem is SWOT analysis which identifies the strengths, weaknesses, opportunity, and threats of the solution.

6. Take action

In the final stage of critical thinking, an evaluation of the solution that should be implemented is conducted. If the solution involves a particular project, a plan of action is implemented to ensure that the solution is executed as initially planned.

The Framework of Critical Thinking

The CT (Critical Thinking) framework follows three main steps which are:
- Clarity
- Conclusions
- Decisions

Clarity

Have you ever found yourself in a situation where you were communicating or discussing an issue with a friend, or a colleague, and you failed to understand their statement? In such a case, you will find yourself continually asking the following questions:
- Could you give more details on that point?
- Could you provide an example?
- Could you discuss that point from another dimension?

Such questions depict that the statement or issue being communicated is not clear enough for the other party, thus not a good base for critical thinking. The problems or issues being addressed are often referred to as headscratchers.

As an individual, before getting down into the critical thinking process, you need to have a clear understanding of what the issue being thought about entails. The problem may be in the form of a goal, project, or an investment. Just as you always have a clear idea about the dress you want to wear, the food you want to eat or the car you want to buy, your critical thinking ideas similarly should be clear. An example of an unclear statement is, "We need to improve our education system." In this case, the problem has not been clearly outlined, and it may be hard to discuss or address the issue. A more precise and realistic statement would be one where the problem is identified, such as, "We need to improve our education system by revising the curriculum being used in our schools."

Critical thinking based on unclear issues often results in poorly made decisions that can affect you in the long term. Ensure that you take enough of your time to analyze your issues of concern to avoid making decisions on unclear grounds. Therefore, clarity is the gate pass to critical thinking.

Conclusions

Just as the name suggests, to conclude means, to sum up, or to end. Having gained a clear picture of what the problem under discussion entails, you as the go-ahead as the decision-maker or part of the decision making to come up with a summary of what you intend to do concerning the problem of discussion. A conclusion is a statement that offers solutions to the issue being discussed. It contains a list of actions that need to be undertaken in the process of solving the identified problem.

Quite often, people often assume that the conclusion and the decisions are the same things. They may be quite similar, but in the thinking process, the two are totally different with different approach techniques. The conclusion here comes before the decision and consists of a list of actions or activities to do which are yet to be implemented.

As a decision-maker, you arrive at the conclusions after critically and logically examining the problem and analyzing any possible solutions. After a successful analysis and the mutual agreement of the parties involved, especially in business meetings, you then come up with a list of possible actions that can be used to handle the problem at hand. From the example above, the conclusion would be, " To revise the curriculum, we need to adopt a new education system and educate the teachers concerning the changes made."

Decisions

You often make decisions daily in your life. You may decide whether to move into a new apartment or just to renovate your old one. You may also choose whether to get married before getting a stable job or to wait until you get the position of your dreams. Basically, you cannot do anything in life without having to make a decision.

Decisions determine the effectiveness of a thinking process. They are made following the conclusions made in the previous step. The main difference that exists between decisions and conclusions which are otherwise used interchangeably is that decisions involve the actual implementation of the list of actions identified in the conclusions process. Making a decision entails determining whether or not you will put listed steps into real-life practices. Based on the example about improving the education system, making the step to train the teachers on the new curriculum changes and its actual implementation is what is termed to as decisions.

Always ensure that the decision you make is in line with the set goals and objectives be it on an individual basis or on a company basis.

Tools for Critical Thinking/Intellectual standards

There are nine universally accepted critical thinking tools, which if adopted, can enhance your critical thinking abilities. These intellectual standards are always used to determine the quality of one's reasoning. They include:

- Clarity
- Accuracy
- Precision
- Relevance
- Depth
- Breadth
- Logical
- Significance
- Fairness

Clarity

In critical thinking, the clarity of a statement is essential. If the statement or problem to be addressed is put in an unclear way, it will be hard to understand it. If unclear statements are used to make decisions, the result is always uncertain. The language used here should be easily understood by the parties involved. Take care of the language and beliefs of the participants to avoid using terms that may bring out contradicting meanings.

You might be wondering how to differentiate between a clear and unclear statement. Here is an example to help you understand the difference.

What needs to be done on the food shortage issue? This question is unclear and somehow tricky to address since one is not aware of what the person asking the question considers to be the problem. Clarity here would be achieved by pointing out the main issue of concern and rephrasing the question to, what does the government need to do to ensure that its citizens have enough food supply and that there is no drought and famine in the country?

The second question is easily understood, making it simple to analyze the causes of drought and famine and possible measures to counter it. A clear problem statement makes the critical thinking process effective. Be sure to make your statement, thoughts, and arguments clear.

To achieve clarity, you can ask the following questions:
- Can you give an example?
- Can you express the statement differently?
- Can you further elaborate on that point?

Accuracy
You may come up with a statement that is clear, but not accurate. You might be wondering how this is possible, but it actually happens in most occasions. The accuracy of a statement is gauged by the way you represent your information with what it actually is in real life. You have to ensure that the information you use is correct and free from errors.

As a critical thinker, before picking any information to use in your argument, you should first ask yourself the following questions:
- Is this information true?
- How and where can I check to confirm if it is true?
- How accurate is this statement?

Such questions will keep you from providing information that lacks a good support base. Most often, you find yourself justifying your facts and ideas saying that they are accurate simply because they came from you and end up seeing those of your opposers as the inaccurate ones. It is therefore advisable that being a critical thinker, you should not force your views or that of a friend to sound accurate while you lack a means of proving that the information is actually valid. Ensure that you use adequate and accurate information to analyze your problem and make viable conclusions.

70% of youths are unemployed.

The above statement seems clear, but it is not accurate for use in an argument. To support is, you may need to look for data on recent research on unemployment rates and use it to support your statement. The use of general statements in arguments is common and sometimes may lead to misinformation in communication and decision making.

Precision
As a critical thinker, you may manage to have a clear and accurate statement, but fail to be precise in it. Precision in critical thinking means that you have included the details necessary to make your statement clear. For example, a statement such as, "Ann is old" is not precise since the old is a general term used to describe age. Different who read or listen to your statement may be left wondering what exactly is denoted by the name old. Old may be taken to mean thirty-five, forty, sixty or even eighty years. Therefore, you need to be clear about the age you denote by saying old. A more precise statement that will be clear to all leaving no room for errors and doubts would be, "Jane is fifty-five years old." If you decide to use units of measurement to give the specifics of

your information, then you should ensure that the units adopted for use are clearly understood by all parties involved.

In case a particular piece of information does not seem precise to you, you may ask the following questions:

- Can you provide additional details?
- Can you be more specific?

Relevance

Relevant information is one that is in line with the issue at hand. Additionally, relevance in critical thinking can be used to describe a situation or a state that can be used to solve the underlying problem. Relevant thinking keeps you as a thinker on the right track towards making a practical decision. It is not uncommon for you, to find that whatever you are thinking is not relevant to the issue at hand and this mostly happens where you lack maximum concentration, and you lack good discipline in thinking.

A good example here is where employees tend to think that the efforts they apply in their work should contribute to a salary raise. Effort does not directly relate to salary or wage, and thus, this argument is irrelevant. Relevance exists where the issues are directly connected.

To be on the safe side when it comes to the relevance of the information you provide, always ask yourself the following simple questions:

- How does this fact connect to the problem at hand?
- How does this idea relate to the previous ones?
- How does your argument relate to the discussion question?

Depth

Just as the name depicts, depth in critical thinking means going deep into the issue at hand. The depth here involves deeply analyzing the problem statement to identify the underlying problems as well as means of handling them intellectually. Lack of in-depth analysis of a theme makes it hard to handle it since its root problems are not identified.

Shallow reasoning and arguments in critical thinking are often linked to the absence of in-depth analysis by the critical thinker. Such can often result in making poor decisions based on shallow arguments and analysis of the subject under discussion. An excellent example of a case in which depth is not sufficiently addressed is, you are asked what needs to be done to reduce the use of drugs in America and you just respond by "Just say no." The answer is so shallow and does not give the question an in-depth analysis.

When it comes to focusing on the depth of your thoughts as a critical thinker, here are some of the questions you need to ask yourself:
- How are the complexities of the question addressed in the answers you give?
- How effectively are you handling the significant issues of concern of the problem under discussion?
- How complex is the question or the statement you have formulated?

Breadth
You may come up with a statement that is clear, precise, accurate, relevant, has good depth but fail to incorporate the aspect of breadth. Breadth in general terms may be used to describe the scope or extent of information. Therefore, when addressing a problem question or statement, ensure that you consider all the relevant viewpoints.

Most often, individuals tend to focus only on their views, forgetting to take into consideration the views of the other party or simply their opponents. You have at one point, or another found yourself ignoring the opposing views since you understand that considering them would likely force you to reconsider your views or arguments. This narrow mindedness results in one settling for things that are in his or her favor. For example, you may not be comfortable sleeping with the lights on, but your roommate prefers to sleep with the lights on because he fears darkness. If you make a decision based on your feelings only then the issue of breadth will not have been addressed. You should also consider your roommate's views and then consent on a mutual decision.

To focus on breadth, here are some of the questions you need to ask yourself as a critical thinker:
- Is there any other way to address this issue?
- How would this argument look from a different point of view?
- Are the views of the other party considered?

Logic
Anytime you think, you tend to bring together different thoughts and ideas. These different thoughts need to be combined in a mutually consistent pattern that makes sense, in such a case, the thinking process is said to be logical. However, it is common for you as an individual to have inconsistent thoughts that are not mutually supportive which are referred to as unlogical thinking. Inconsistency of thoughts and ideas comes as a result of the conflicting beliefs that exist in your mind.

A good example here is, an employer analyzing the performance of his employees and ascertaining that additional training needs to be done to boosts their performance. Despite the evidence, he concludes that there is no need for workshops and seminars for the employees. The conclusion does not logically follow the evidence.

Some of the questions that tend to help make whatever you are thinking logical include:
- Do all these views or arguments logically fit together?
- Does this point of view make sense?
- Does the argument flow in line with what you previously said?

Significance

As a critical thinker, your point of view should be most relevant to the issue being addressed. When thinking, you tend to take into account most of the aspects that you consider relevant to the topic under discussion but often fail to understand that not all of the relevant information is equally important in the process.

An example to help you understand the aspect of significance is how most students fail to focus on the significant questions such as, what do I need to become an educated youth? But instead, focus on less significant issues such as what do I need to get an A in this subject?

Determining the most significant points to consider among the many relevant ones is not as simple as it may sound. Here are some of the questions that may guide you in this:
- How is that point of view significant in the context?
- Which is the most important information needed to handle the issue?
- Which of the view, ideas, or concepts is more significant?

Fairness

As a critical thinker, you should always consider coming up with justified thoughts or decisions. These are thoughts that have been made fairly in context. Fairness here means that you should not only stand for the ideas or views that will work out well in your favor. You should also consider the implications of your thoughts on other people. You should not be a selfish thinker.

Here is an example to help you understand fairness. You live with a roommate who cannot concentrate in studies with the music on, but you always put the music on claiming that it consoles your mind and argue that if your roommate wants to study, he should visit the library. The reasoning here is not fair since it is centered on the interests of one party.

- To achieve fairness, you can put into use the following questions.
- Is my approach to the issue fair, or is it centered on my own interests?
- What will be the implication of my thoughts on others?
- Are the viewpoints represented sympathetically?

Intellectual Traits

Having to apply standards of thinking to critical thinking elements develops intellectual traits, which include:

- Intellectual courage
- Intellectual humility
- Intellectual empathy
- Intellectual autonomy
- Intellectual integrity
- Intellectual Perseverance
- Fair-mindedness
- Confidence in Reason

Chapter 3: Benefits of Critical Thinking

Critical thinking is a very significant concept that is not only relevant to the realm of academics but also a critical real-life model, which is used to build efficient and successful problem solving skills. The technique involves the application of logic to enhance more reasonable decision-making. The key benefits of critical thinking include:

Understanding different approaches to a problem. With critical thinking, you will automatically become aware of the different approaches to every situation, including the ability to assess those approaches. Instead of relying on a uniform standard method of problem solving, you can learn how to identify more valuable approaches, which increases success in problem solving.

Save time. With critical thinking, you will be able to have a time-saving mindset. You will learn that not every information is important when evaluating a problem. You will be able to filter out relevant from irrelevant information. Critical thinking teaches you how to invest your time and resources only on essential tools. This also ensures that you only consider the best decision.

Critical thinking enables you to appreciate differing worldviews. Critical thinking enables you to develop empathy, which opens your mind for different points of views. You will be able to see beyond and never judge arguments based on cultural norms or other differing factors. This understanding and empathy are very key to leadership and effective teamwork.

Critical thinking enhances communication. By building and analysing your evidence for every given premise, you will become an effective communicator. Critical thinking enables u to develop relevant points that support your arguments and enhances your communication.

Critical thinking promotes decision-making. Critical thinking transforms one's ability to make decisions. You will be able to abandon guesswork and intuition decision-making and begin to adopt more analytical methods of making sound decisions

Increased ability to reason. As a critical thinker, you will be able to become a more balanced problem solver. You will also become aware of two reasoning types, inductive and deductive, and know when to apply them. Grounding decisions makes the effectual process of solving problems.

Qualities of a Good Critical Thinker

Good critical thinkers demonstrate the following qualities:
- Inquisitiveness in regards to diverse issues
- Interested to become well-informed
- Attentive to situations that promote critical thinking
- Self-confidence in his/her ability to think
- Open-mindedness when it comes to world views
- Alertness to possible future events with the aim of anticipating consequences
- Listening and understanding the opinion of others
- Honesty in facing self stereotypes, prejudices, and biases
- Prudence in alternating, making or suspending judgements

When to Apply Critical Thinking

The previous section has discussed the importance of critical thinking and definitions of critical thinking. There has been a lot of evolution that may force you to think most of the time critically. Critical thinking has been helpful to many, but it is not recommended to be applied every time. You have to not only know where to apply critical thinking but also when to use it.

There is a rule to decide on whether to use critical thinking in a particular situation when the answer to a problem, initiative, goal, or circumstance is significant. Therefore, you can use critical thinking when the outcome makes a substantial difference in your industry or individual position i.e., a casual mail about where to go out for dinner can't be appalling if there is a miscommunication. A misunderstood mail about the requirements of a right or customer problem may have far-reaching implications. Due to this, you may be forced to at least use critical thinking on the mail that describes a customer's problem as divergent to mails about dinner.

Below is a list of examples on where and when you might be forced to use critical thinking. The list has been divided into three, and the first list contains high-level business functions, the second list includes specific business goals, and the third list contains daily activities that many people use in improving business visons. When you have critical thinking tools, you can easily add the list with your areas of a specification to your job.

Critical thinking mostly come up in job descriptions, resumes, CV writing, and desirable characteristics. There are different ways on when to use critical thinking in high-level business functions as follows:

- When a project proposal has milestones with particular dates and deliverables, yet individuals aren't able to beat the time frame given.
- There is a change in norm without any detailed explanation.
- Metrics being tracked aren't able to give guidance of improving the predicted result.

- When you make a call to determine the origin of a problem, and you have an unexpected answer.
- The delivered goods don't concur with bills or expenses.
- Increment in expenses and they don't match decrement investments in reduction.
- Data conclusions aren't adding up or making sense.
- There is a slope in the graph of a good that has been projected.
- Customers are coming up with complaints about rates that are significantly dissimilar from what you have dignified.

To Improve Something

- Decreasing customer care cost by 25 percent and increasing customer contentment.
- Increasing productivity.
- You are enhancing communication between your department and others.
- Helps in the determination of how to change marketing plans and be much competitive.
- Increase your business growth.
- Decrease costs by 25 percent.
- You are finding and hiring more qualified and professional candidates.
- Determine what to expect with the ever-growing health care charges.
- Shortening of development times by a third.
- You are decreasing the meantime to repair by 20 percent.
- Shortening of order to delivery by half.

- We are increasing the quality of products to increase customer ratings.
- We are improving the advertising campaigns outcome.

Critical thinking to be used in the future you have to consider:

- How can you develop a new good that can bring competition with the new operations now that it has been brought about?
- Two significant employees just left- now what?
- Your legacy good that gives the majority of your incomes and revenue has high wear and tear rate. What should you do?
- How can you avoid an unpleasant event from happening again?
- How can you imitate what you did for the next period?
- Are you willing to build or buy your way to enlarge your provision contribution?
- How can you expand your financial strategy?
- Having a budget, how can you achieve your goals?
- How do you increase the progression of your occupation?

Specific Daily Activities Where Critical Thinking Can Be Used

- Assembling and fixing of something
- Attendance of meetings
- Assessment of risks
- Coaching
- Conducting brainstorming classes

When to Use Critical Thinking

- Creation and interpretation of surveys
- Create presentations
- Engage in planning financial activities
- Engage in face to face talks
- Proposal evaluation
- Making of go on no go pronouncements
- Organization
- Calendar planning
- Speech preparation
- Prioritization
- Reading to pay attention to the underlying words
- Contract review
- Spreadsheet review
- Setting of goals
- Metric setting
- Teaching
- Writing of emails, directions, proposals, and reports
- Writing and conduction of enactment appraisals.

Critical thinking can be used in almost every place in your business and life activities, but you must be selective. You can choose to use essential thinking only when you think the result will bring out or make some variance. Critical thinking intends to identify reliable info and make reliable complements. It comprises of mindset skills which can be enhanced through the understanding of significant perceptions, training, and request. There are very many stages that strengthen the development of a critical thinker:

- Stage one: unreflective thinker

- Stage two: challenged thinker
- Stage three: beginning thinker
- Stage four: practicing thinker
- Stage five: advanced thinker
- Stage six: master thinker

You can develop all these steps only if you; accept there are problems in our thinking and start a regular practice.

Chapter 4: Routines to Improve Critical Thinking

There are some routines which if you continuously practice, can significantly improve your critical thinking skills. Such routine practices include the following:

Taking Deep Breaths

Participating in daily deep belly breathing or brain breaks can significantly help you focus on your attention better. Not only does it increase focus and concentration, but it also enhances daily happiness and increases your levels of calm while decreasing stress and anxiety. Deep breathing slows the heart rate, lowers the blood pressure, and sharpens your mind's ability to focus-all of which are crucial for a capable critical thinker.

Deep breathing also helps you to control your emotions, and you will handle situations which high emotional consequences calmly, you tend to think clearly and feel issues better when you are calm. Moreover, when you take time to breathe slowly in and out, you evoke a relaxation response that both calms and invigorates you. It will help you to function better during the day and sleep better during the night.

Studies have shown that controlled breathing increases your alertness, reduce stress, and boost your immune system. It also improves your concentration levels and improves your vitality. These are vital skills of a capable critical thinker.

Be A Keen Reader And A Sound Synthesizer Information

A competent critical thinker is always striving to get new information daily so as to be up to date and be well informed on what is happening in your surroundings. The best way to remain informed always is to actively read materials touching on a wide range of topics from various sources. You should then combine the information from the multiple sources and add your analysis of the literature of the subject you are handling-this is what is referred to as synthesis. By synthesizing, it means that you understand what you are reading and you can provide new interpretation or analysis of those sources.

For you to synthesize information better, you should always evaluate the accuracy and truthfulness of statements, claims, and information you read and hear. Once you master the art of evaluation, you will be able to separate facts from fiction and accurate from misleading. You should consider the information analytically and critically, and you must ask yourself questions about the source of information. Find out whether the sources are experts in the given area and whether quality research can back up the information or the opinion you are reading. You sharpen your critical skills when you question the information you are presented with in a purposeful, intentional, and frequent manner.

Practice Self-talk

A positive self-talk is a powerful tool for increasing your confidence and controlling negative emotions. If you master positive self-talk, you end up being more confident, motivated, and productive.

Your thoughts are the source of your emotions and mood. The conversations you have with yourself can be destructive or beneficial. They influence how you feel about yourself and how you respond to situations in your life.

Self-talk is our inner voice or monologue. It is how we plan, problem solve, practice critical thinking and reflect.

Positive self-talk usually consists of words which inspire, motivate air to remind us to focus and keep moving. Find out the last thing you said to yourself and whether it was positive or negative. You need to practice positive self-talk to stay inspired, motivated and focused on critical thinking.

Practice Goal Setting

Setting your goals is very crucial if you want to live a successful and fulfilling life. When you have goals, you tend to push yourself into achieving them. Critical thinkers are prudent and patient when setting goals for themselves. Set goals and then look at it from a SMART perspective. Set goals which are specific, measurable, attainable, realistic, and which can be achieved within a particular timeframe. Be willing to start small and work your way up to complete your vision as a capable critical thinker.

Know Your Weaknesses

Everybody has strengths and weaknesses, so are you. To be a practical critical thinker, you should always find out if there is something you need to improve and start taking small steps to do so. For example, if you want to become a better listener, then you need to learn how you can avoid being impatient and overbearing when others are talking. If you want to improve your critical thinking skills, recognize your weaknesses and make a proactive plan to develop and act on them.

Travel Widely

Good critical thinkers never stop learning. There is no better way to gain new knowledge and experiences than by traveling extensively. There is always something new to discover, no matter where we are in life. Being a learner of life keeps your mind fresh and young. Traveling widely, therefore, is a crucial critical thinking habit to possess. Once you have acquired information out there, you need to combine it with relevant action. To reinforce what you have learned, practice and play with your new skills to cement the learning into your brain.

Best Practices for Improving Critical Thinking Skills

Don't waste time

Capable critical thinkers never engage in activities or events which waste their time. You should always strive to use your time productively. For you to and time wastage, always ensure you plan well your day in advance. Practice strategic planning in order not to waste your time. Avoid living reactively as this may put you out of control of your life. You should also monitor your time. Try measuring your time for a week or even a day. This will help you identify portions of poorly used time after which you can take decisive actions to correct it.

You should also learn to prioritize your day. Allocate more time to the essential things which have a significant impact on your life.

Learn new things every day

As an excellent critical thinker, you should always aim at learning something new each day. Be curious about your world and be aware of how much you have to learn daily. Studies show that learning a new thing each day helps improve your brain's performance on several tasks and helps you to learn even better. It also enhances your learning speed. Your brains neurons are stimulated when it receives new information. More neural pathways are formed, and electrical impulses travel faster across them as you attempt to process further information. The more channels that are created, the faster impulses can move, and the better you become a critical thinker.

Have a questioning mind

A questioning mind is an essential tool of critical thinking. The ideal critical thinker possesses a questioning mind. The key to powerful thinking is by asking questions. When you ask questions, you succeed as a critical thinker. Questioning forms new patterns in the brain. The more patterns it develops, the more flexible it becomes. With flexibility, it can access information already stored in your mind.

Practice active listening

A good critical thinker is an active listener. Active listening can be acquired and developed with practice. You need to fully concentrate on what is being said rather than passively hearing the message of the speaker. It involves listening with all senses and giving your full attention to the speaker. Avoid distractions when others are talking. Practice useful none verbal skills such as maintaining eye contact, nodding, asking questions when you are engaging in a conversation with others. Active listening helps you to remember better the details of the information you hear. It also aids your understanding of better critical thinking.

How to improve critical thinking skills in college

Critical thinking skills take time, patience, and practice to develop and grow. If you are a college student, you need to practice the following to build and strengthen your critical thinking skills:

Be self-aware

To improve your critical thinking skills, you need to be self-aware. You need to change some of your long-standing practices, behaviors, beliefs. To critically engage with theories, ideas, and work of others, you need to develop self-awareness. Find out what motivates you and your core values.

Form or join a study group

Research shows that students who participate in discussions with others on various topics improve their critical thinking skills. Discussion groups expose you to different opinions, approaches, and feelings of others.

Join a debating society

Debates serves to enlighten you better. You can also gain new knowledge from the debating floor. Studies show that debate is a valuable tool to improve your critical thinking skills.

Attend essential seminars of thinking and training

If your course gives you the option of taking critical thinking, sign up for the. Critical thinking can be taught and learned. You can also look out for upcoming seminars and workshops on critical thinking. it could be one great way to improve your critical thinking skills.

Engage critically with your course content

When completing your assignment, ask yourself whether you have gone beyond demonstrating a basic understanding of the topical. You need to analyze your argument and synthesize all the available information before you draw your conclusions.

Chapter 5: Techniques, Strategies, And Skills

Strategies for Developing Critical Thinking in Students

Famous psychologist, Lawrence Balter insists on the reason as to why children should grow up being critical in their conclusions. Coming up with a big group of same-minded characters with a powerful feeling of studying is not the main objective of education. There is a Chinese philosopher who once said that "learning without thought is labor lost," this means that thinking without learning is dangerous. If you want to enhance and have new astonishing clarifications to the overabundance of difficulties within you, then you must allow teachers to develop critical thinking in students starting from a tender age. Below are ways in which teachers can help in developing critical thinking skills in students that can be of help to them in the future and their lives.

Open-ended questions
Breaking of rote learning is essential, but at times you are forced to break that monotony. You will do this by asking students open questions that will force them to think. You can take an example where a history teacher is asking students reasons to why a specific bill was passed in an assembly by making them get the point of making the contribution and having different opinions from them.

Solving of problems
You can challenge your students with a tricky question; thus this will help in boosting their critical thinking abilities. It will help them make use of the properties they have and yield creative resolutions. Give them a problem they can relate with like when it's a math question, connect it to the journey they take to school or anything revolving around school operations can be a better option.

Inspire creativity

You can have a convention where you make students study a fixed formula created to resolve a problem. This can limit their creative essence and make them lose hope in using their information or data. You can try something like asking them to give recommendations for catalyst speeding up a chemical production can be a favorable option. They will be going through various incentives and evaluate their properties. When it comes to younger kids, you can use playtime and learning that can be very productive.

Interactive games

We can refer to these games as brain or mind games as they push a player to think hard and fast for them to win. Having a reward will be attractive and will make them keep going and practice critical thinking. You can have a lot of choices at free thinking games and superb minds. When you have games with rewards, then it can be excellent in motivating and developing critical thinking.

Impart Independence

Any time you will be giving your students answers to questions, then they will depend on you for all responses. This can affect them, and they won't perform well in examinations or tests, or where a question is twisted differently. Allow them to think on their own to help them understand creativeness.

Ultimate examples

Someone starting a class can fail to understand what critical thinking involves, so you have to give examples to help understand easily. You can tell the beginners how critical thinkers have been able to resolve problems efficiently and how they have been rewarded for their capabilities.

Classification

You have to make your students know to organize their unplanned opinions. From this point is when you will bring in rating. Make them practice how to sort their problems in groups, and this will make them be able to assess the ones that can work out the best in their situations.

Vocabulary lessons

By sparking internal creative process of students, the brain isn't enough. You must teach your students how to express themselves. Once the students have organized the issues they have in their minds, teach them essential terms such as accurate, authority, rational, bias among many others.

Mind connections

When your students are learning to plan their minds to brainstorm give them hope to discover the relationships amid their ideas. They have to summarize ideas, have a comparison of points, find similarities, measure differences, and get to know why a good chosen answer is right. There can tell me more than one correct answer.

Demonstrations

Having examples of critical thinkers is very inspiring and to achieve such then you have to show your students how it's done. Have practical events of issue identification, weighing of pros and cons, and finally getting to a logical decision.

Productive debates

Involve your students in a discussion that will allow them to show and test their critical thinking skills. This will give them ground to argue out on their own and get to know their weakness and of others, among other things.

Peer assessment

Creating competition among the students with their peers will make sense that they are supposed to interact based on critical thinking amongst themselves. When they bounce off ideas, then they will learn to distinguish the advantages and disadvantages of each other's opinion and make conclusions independent of their thinking.

How To Teach Critical Thinking In Schools

Critical thinking skills are gaining importance in elementary education, and teaching them can be a challenge for teachers in schools. On how we evaluate essential skills of thinking and incorporate it into our daily lessons is critical, and it needs such expertise:

Connect various ideas

Put together many ideas is vital in teaching critical thinking. For instance, school teachers can ask students about who takes a bus to work, and if there is one, why should it be of the essence to have a training program. Such questions will assist students in having considerations about various situations and solutions that can help in getting the knowledge to new contexts.

Brainstorming

This an excellent tool to help in enhancing education. It's also an excellent tool in critical thinking exercise more so when putting together visual elements that come along with original thinking and classroom interactions.

Incorporation of various points of view

This is one of the best exercises for students to use in exploring concepts from multiple perspectives. This process will not only establish how an idea should be assessed from various points of view, but it will also give learners chance to share their opinions while also getting something new from the others as they listen and interact.

Teaching Strategies For Critical Thinking Skills

Thinking critically is not about thinking only but about thinking independently too. Most students who have mastered critical thinking skills can be advantaged to single out effects that can shape their personality and impacts that cannot. You need a few strategies to enhance critical thinkers.

1. Have questioning techniques

Have a question which is an essential tool to improve critical thinking skills. This strategy is straightforward and can be easily enhanced by students. Create items that will give students extra thinking ability. Ask questions which have a yes or no answer. Such issues will provide people with platforms to gauge their knowledge to a topic. Ask inquiries that can make them think more deep-seated however much frustrations it will bring.

2. Student-led discussions

Student learning environments support critical thinking skills by requiring students to reflect metacognitively. In a classroom, students will depend on their peers to have answers to their questions than a teacher. You can use mystery game where students depend on their own to get answers. It is a fantastic process because you see how students are interacting in learning. This will make them be focused throughout the lesson, and they can't even realize the teacher is in class. The process will make the experience so powerful and excellent for engaging student's collaboration.

3. Inquiry-based learning

Students should have an interest in what they are studying. Learning full of inquiry is essential as it involves students to grow in the learning process and engage in critical thinking skills. This learning process consists of more than students learning, but also activating concentration and interest. To have successful inquiry learning, you have to create questions they will want answers to. Students should be able to ask high-order thinking questions.

4. Collaboration

An essential aspect of critical thinking is the capability to ask questions and scrutinize them. When students have a partnership with their peers, it promotes building character of their own that enhances independence and critical thinking. You should have time throughout the lesson and help them converse with peers and exchange ideas. It assists students in learning amongst themselves, thus can help in eliminating confusion and misunderstandings. The collaboration will help in expansion of students thinking by showing that everyone has a different thinking capability.

5. Problem-based studying

This strategy gives students hope to enact critical thinking skills by giving them structure for discovery that assists students have a deeper understanding. The steps are easy and can be used repeatedly for new topics.

- Exploring specific issue or difficulty.
- Researching and brainstorming.
- Developing solutions and presenting them to the class.
- Creation of call to action and the steps to be followed.

Chapter 6: Types of Critical Thinking

Logical reasoning (or only "logic" for short) is one of the pillars of critical thinking. It works by bringing up issues like:

- ☒ If this is true, what else must be true?
- ☒ If this is true, then what else is most likely true?
- ☒ If this is not true, what else cannot be true?

These are all inferences: they are associations between a given statement (the "premise") and some other statement (the "conclusion"). Inferences are the essential structures of logical thinking. Strict principles governing what is considered a valid inference and what does not- it is just like math applied to sentences as opposed to numbers.

Example: If there is somebody at the entryway, the pooch will bark.

Expecting this sentence holds true, some different sentences must likewise be valid.

1. If the pooch did not bark, there is nobody at the entryway.
2. Because the pooch barked does not mean there is somebody at the entryway.

There are likewise a couple of sentences that are most likely valid, for example,

1. The pooch can detect (hear or smell) when somebody is at the entryway.
2. The pooch belongs with the individuals who live in the house where the entryway is found.

Logical Reasoning

There are three main kinds of logic, each characterized by its own type of inference.

A deduction is when the conclusion, based on the premises, must be valid. For instance, if the facts demonstrate that the pooch always barks when somebody is at the entryway, and the facts confirm that there is somebody at the entryway, then the facts must prove that the canine will bark. Reality is messy and does not always fit in with the constraints of deductive reasoning (there are most likely no pooches who always bark when somebody is at the entryway). Deductive thinking is as yet significant in fields like law, engineering, and science, where strict facts still hold. All math is deductive.

Induction is the point at which the conclusion, given the premises, is most likely. The appropriate responses are less conclusive than they are in deductive reasoning, yet they are usually more useful. Induction is our only method for predicting what will occur later on: we look at how things are, and how they have been previously, and we make an informed prediction about what will likely happen.

All predictions, however, depend on probability, not certainty: for instance, it is highly probable that the sun will rise tomorrow morning. However, it is not guaranteed, since there is a wide range of calamities that could occur from now till then.

Abduction is when the conclusion is the best guess. It commonly starts with a fragmented arrangement of observations and continues to the likeliest conceivable explanation. Abductive thinking yields the sort of everyday decision-making that does its best with the information at hand, which is almost always incomplete. A medical diagnosis is an example of abductive reasoning: given a set of symptoms, which diagnosis best explains most- if not all- of them? A patient might be asleep or fail to report all the symptoms, making the evidence incomplete. A medical practitioner must give a diagnosis which might fail to cover all the symptoms.

Scientific Reasoning

Scientific reasoning is the pillar supporting the whole structure of logic underlying scientific research. It is challenging to investigate the entire process, in any detail, because the precise nature changes between the different scientific disciplines.

Four fundamental establishments underlie the thought, pulling together the cycle of scientific reasoning.

Observation

Most research has observation as its underlying structure. Observing natural phenomena is the thing that leads a specialist to address what is happening and start to define scientific questions and hypotheses. Any hypothesis and theories should be examined against observable data.

Theories and Hypotheses

In this stage, the researcher proposes the possible reasons for the phenomena, the laws of nature controlling the behavior. Scientific research uses different scientific reasoning procedures to touch base at a practical research issue and theory. A hypothesis is, for the most part, separated into individual theories, or problems, and tested steadily.

Predictions

A good researcher needs to predict the aftereffects of their research, expressing their thoughts regarding the result of the trial, frequently as an alternative hypothesis. Scientists more often than not test the prediction of a hypothesis or theory, instead of the thesis itself. If the predictions are observed to be mistaken, then the hypothesis is inaccurate or needing refinement.

Data

Data is the applied piece of science, and the consequences of accurate observations are tested against the predictions. If the observations collaborate with the predictions, the hypothesis is reinforced. If not, the theory should be changed. A scope of factual tests is used to test predictions, albeit numerous observation-based scientific disciplines cannot use statistics.

The Psychology of Critical Thinking

Social psychology is old; however, the science depicted in these pages is current. The facts demonstrate that we owe a lot to logicians like Aristotle, Socrates, Plato, and many others, who thought about society and made astute observations. Later researchers anyway have since put vast numbers of these early thoughts, to the empirical test. We, as a whole, have a social legacy to which we are obliged for some contemporary ideas.

Psychologists concur that there is no single right approach to examine how individuals think or behave. There are, in any case, different schools of thought that advanced all through the development of psychology that keeps on molding how we explore human behavior. For instance, a few therapists may credit specific behavior to biological factors, for example, hereditary qualities while another therapist should think about early youth encounters to be a more probable explanation for the behavior. These different ideas contributed to the dominant theories which today impact and direct social psychological research and ideas.

Theoretical Domain

These early scholars proposed general ideas this way upheld as clarifying all social conduct. For instance, some recommended that hedonism explains all that we do. Other masterminds proposed that we comprehend human behavior merely as a component of impersonation or impulses. This emphasis on broad ideas presented the issue of "nominalism" into psychology. Do we truly understand more by merely observing behavior? In the end, social analysts perceived the deficiency of sweeping standards and started the improvement of hypotheses dependent on the scientific method.

What characterizes social brain science as an order? As it were, social psychology is the scientific research of social cognition (how individuals think about one another), how individuals are affected by the behavior of others (for instance conformity), and how they identify with one another through participation or hostility. This rationale brought about noteworthy theories in psychology, and a few in sociology and other related disciplines.

Learning theories
These speculations incorporate old classical conditioning, operant conditioning, and observational learning. Of these methodologies, the most notable for psychology is observational learning. For instance, we figure out how to be aggressive, we figure out how to fight, to hurt each other, by watching others acting in these ways. We build up our attitudes, our emotions of hostility, and other social practices through the unobtrusive and open observation of others. Guardians are good examples in early development, yet others, including teachers and friends, additionally impact children. In recent times the media has assumed a significant role, and a lot of research has been directed, because of TV, on human behavior.

Social cognition

Cognitive consistency theories are essential points of view on social psychology. These points of view propose the possibility that individuals have a necessary requirement for cognitive consistency and balance. For example, when individuals become mindful of beliefs and attitudes conflicting with their behavior, this inconsistency is experienced as an uncomfortable emotional state. Dissonance, thus, inspires social change and a revamping of beliefs and attitudes.

Information Processing

Advanced information theories influenced advanced theory development in social cognition in natural sciences. Social cognition theories find the reasons for human conduct in the preparation of information, and in our endeavors to understand others and ourselves. The fundamental thought is that we function like human PCs as we encode data, store it in memory, and recover it at a moment's notice.

Equity and Exchange Theories

It ought not to astonish us that social psychology theories mirror our financial framework, although that remaining parts an implicit presumption of value and trade theories. Aspiring for equity and fair results reflect ideal economic relations in a capitalist society. Basically, these hypotheses clarify human social conduct as far as rewards, expenses, and profits, proposing that all relationships contain these three components. Bringing up a child can be fulfilling, yet additionally, provide many costs not immediately evident to young parents. The rewards may include the psychological satisfaction of creating and nurturing life. The expenses can consist of the undeniable economic expenditures, yet also, psychological costs if the child is troublesome and picks an opposed path of conduct.

Methodology Domain

How would we study social conduct? Social psychology as a science is based on two techniques. The first procedure is a correlation, for example, analyzing the quality and direction of relationships between factors on topics of interest. The second is experimental research in the lab, based on the control of independent factors observing for consequences for dependent factors.

Correlational research

For instance, we can study the rate of lung cancer among smokers. If smoking expands the danger of disease, we ought to anticipate a relationship between the degree of smoking and the incidence of cancer. It is important to remember that correlation does not equal causation. However, for progressively specific issues, random sampling empowers the analyst to reach inferences about opinions in the all-inclusive community.

The survey method remains a significant apparatus for social psychology in fields of opinion research and attitude scaling. It is more mainstream in the part of social psychology found in sociology. The experimental method, however, searching for cause and effect still has the consideration of most social analysts in psychology.

Experimental research

This kind of research is commonly held in a controlled situation like a laboratory. From the earliest starting point, psychology was built upon the natural sciences with goals to one day become develop as a discipline. Given the short recorded time since the start of social psychology, it is too soon to assess its prosperity as natural science. However, the yearning to turn into an acceptable scientific discipline explains the techniques used by most social psychologists. Experimental research is riddled with challenges such as bias in experiments and ethics in preliminary investigations.

Practical Domain

As has been appeared, social psychology is keen on an entire scope of social issues. What are the as of now significant social inquiries? An ongoing social issue of significance is the impact of violence in the media on aggression in society. In the United States, thousands are killed every year by acts of terrorism. Sometimes the discussion on violence is distorted, for example, by the argument of the gun lobby that firearms do not kill people, but people kill people. Such thinking is oversimplified and ignores the way that the accessibility of weapons is a stimulus that routinely prompts fatal encounters in a society where violence is underestimated. The impact of TV violence remains a significant social issue, and applied research into this subject may deliver impactful social solutions.

If it is challenging to create a pure science as observed in the natural sciences, many research findings can inform and build valuable applied knowledge. Research on attitudes, may, for example, be invaluable in advertising and in persuading public opinion. Obviously, we must be mindful of the line between persuasion and manipulation; a line that is often disregarded in the advertising world of today. Also, research on bias might be valuable in managing and resolving issues of ethnic and national hostility.

A significant issue in social psychology is whether discoveries found in the recreation of life in laboratories can, in truth, apply to real-life experiences. Do individuals behave similarly, in real-life situations as under the created conditions set by the experimenter?

When the situation demands it, it is possible to apply many of the laboratory findings to the real world. For example, a case study of university students showed that half of them tortured their cohorts in prison cells. This example relates to many real-life examples of torture and human rights violations. And such use of applications must be the general basis of significant research finding and theory in social psychology.

Chapter 7: Exercise For Critical Thinking

In this chapter, we will handle topics such as:
- ➤ Time to think critically
- ➤ Analysis of Facts and Applying Logic
- ➤ Critical Thinking Exercise
- ➤ Powerful Skills Related to Critical Thinking

Time To Think Critically

When you have the capability to transform good understanding it can be considered as a way of critical thinking because it is transforming an individual's lifestyle. You should be able to ask and follow the outline of inquiry to its logical ending, despite having odds with strong beliefs, there should be a powerful tool in self-discovery.

How To Make Your Decision

In our day to day lives, you have to make decisions on what to wear, eat or how to spend your time. Making of decision is a no-brainer, and you have to make a choice even if it's not the finest choice because latent significances are hardly worth to toil for. Many of the times you have to make some difficult decisions like:
- When do I move?
- What kind of job suits you best?
- Are you in the right relationship?
- Should you proceed with the divorce?

You may have a lot of decisions to think about thus making the brain to be muddled due to the hard decisions you are trying to make. The more time you consume in making decision, the more you will get confused, and stuck feeling wasted. The confusion may make you so uncomfortable that you ignore being associated with making of such tough decisions. You are not advised to overthink as it will affect your process of making decisions. Don't over task your brain by trying to predict the future despite the certainty of the results. Life is full of surprises, and you have to be certain of making the right decision which depends on your faith. When you decide to make a great decision, then you have to learn on taking many steps incorporated with a huge dose of emotive direction. In short, you have to start reasoning first before listening to the heart. Below are some main reasons on how to make decisions without any regret:

1.   Have a vision in life

Having a vision in life should be the key factor and reference point in every decision you are about to or going to make. When you have a dream. Where do you see your life depending on your career options, relationship, financial stability, lifestyle among others? What plans do you have to enhance your vision? You have to note down your visions and values in life that define your character and go through them any time you are free. With your visions nicely planned even when you have a tough decision to make you will have it easy due to the planning you have. Without the plan then you will be stressed and regret a lot of decisions. Make your choices based on your vision and have the closest alignment with your plan.

2.   Evaluation of Pros and Cons

When making a decision, you have to consider the consequences it will enact whether positive or negative. Note down a list of pros and cons for every substitute and give each point a priority having the most important one topping the list. What are the possibilities of your cons? Are they better than your pros? Are you able to cope up with negativity fallout or significances? What are you capable of doing to moderate the upshot?

3.   Calling a friend

Take your time to select two of your friends who you value their opinion and judgment whenever you interact with them. Talk to them about the visions you have in life and share with them the list of your pros and cons and request for their contribution to your decision. A friend who will have a different opinion can help you in having the right decisions. Having a personal coach can be a great advantage because you can be challenged by requests to answer questions about your motivation, feelings, and wants.

4. Raise a higher power

Get a quiet place, take a deep breath, close your eyes, then pray and meditate, and ask for direction. Your inner wisdom and intuition will rise your thinking, and by the time you cool down the disturbing confusion of overthinking decision. Put yourself in your own world and think about your life and concentrate on how you feel. You must have somewhere to write down how you feel after reflecting and then give it a few days. You can be surprised by the unexpected present answers.

5. Attempt the coin trick

This idea is great as it brings everything you touch with your needs. Take a quarter and allocate one decision choice to heads and other to tails. Flip the coin, and formerly it lands, concentrate on the side you chose hoping it lands on that side. Wherever there are more choices you have to balance the choices against each other by the trick. This is the reaction that you can easily do. You will have something that will push you within your heart, and you have to check on the answer with a lot of strictness. You have to make the choices despite the conflicts considering your deepest needs.

6. Research and experiment

You have to do some work to have some knowledge about your options. Investigate and ask questions, interact with people who have been in the same situation. Try experimenting with its outcomes and when you want to move, have a straight decision. If you have a job chance, get permission to shadow someone in the office. In situations where you want to end a relationship, you are encouraged to take time before making up your mind on the decision.

7. No looking back

After finishing your work, honoring your vision, examining your pros and cons, seeking guidance, and making a choice then you have to make the decision and don't look at your past. In life you have a million paths you can take, and they all lead to various prospects and potential significances. There is no guarantee, but you have to access one. You have to consider uncertainty as part of the adventure. Having consideration of this adventure you will have confidence in whatever you decide and have to move forward. You have to learn on every path you follow. The ability to come up with decisions is the boost for professional growth. When you get into a decision with the knowledge that uncertainty is unacceptable and you have to decide without fear of getting stuck. When you take the steps discussed above then you will empower yourself and have no room to regret.

Analysis Facts And Applying Logic

You have to keep in mind that critical thinking is an active design of thinking. After receiving messages ad assuming them, you can still consider the as saying. You can inquire if the messages are finely supported. When you consider critical thinking in messages that you will be putting into consideration a variety of skills such as: paying attention, exploration, evaluation, inference, interpretation, explanation and self-regulation. When you lack an open-minded brain then you can never be a better success.

Listening

For you to have a better understanding of listening, you must know the difference amid listening and hearing. Hearing is the psychological process of getting sounds while listening is the psychological means of converting a sense of sounds. In our daily life, we are surrounded by a lot of various uproars and sounds. If you try to make sense out the sounds then you can spend the whole day doing it. Despite the many sounds we hear, a lot of them are filtered out. There are some noises that will pass to the frontline of your consciousness. As you listen you also make sense out of the sounds. This happens daily subconsciously, without keeping in mind about the process.

Critical thinking requires you to carefully listen to messages. You have to be careful of what is said and not said. You have to be keen not to be disrupted by any noise messing up with the ideas you had. At that moment whatever you need is just the message. Listening can be difficult when the message being conveyed has charged info. Take an example where you are trying to discuss abortion. You will listen as the other person speaks but there will be a strong feeling forcing you to start an argument. At the end you will find that both of you will talk past each other thus there will be no one listening.

Analysis

After listening to a message, you can analyze it. You can as well analyze messages at the same time you are listening. When you analyze something, there will be consideration that it's greater detail and separates major components of the message. You are acting like a surgeon on the message, bringing out all various components and putting them out for advance contemplation and possible action.

Evaluation

When you evaluate a task, you will be going on with the progression of analysis by checking on different statements and opinions for legitimacy. A way that you can evaluate a message is by questioning what is being said and by who. The following is an outline of questions you may ask:

Is the speaker credible?

You may not be an expert in a certain field you are supposed to talk about, but with the research you can be a mini-expert.

With common sense does the statement sound to be true or false?

It may sound fishy, but having more than four glasses of wine in a table may seem not to be right. It can be seen as binge drinking.

Does the logic employed holds up study?

When you consider Shonda's speech you might realize the logic part of her. But later on her speech there are a few misconceptions.

What objections are raised by the message?

Adding to the probability of Shonda's suggestion being binge drinking, it also brings the leeway of enhancing alcoholism or long term fitness complications.

Can further information affect the message?

A lot of info or data will not be in agreement with her claims. When you research you will find out that most medical outcome disagrees with claims that drinking more glasses of wine daily is a good thing.

Critical Thinking Exercise

Factual critical thinking exercise seek honesty. You have to be daring and independent thinking from conventional thoughts and discover unfound truth. Critical thinking has also been considered as the heart of dispelling bigger myths about our world and how it's bringing a lot of changes to the world. Critical thinking differs from analytical and lateral thinking likely: analytical thinking aims at reviewing the info you presented. Lateral thinking aims at putting data to a different context. Critical thinking targets to create general judgment about data which is free and has no false premises.

Critical thinking has been considered to be difficult to grasp as it requires students to keep aside assumptions and beliefs to study and think without being biased or judging. It involves postponing beliefs you have just to explore and question topics from blank pages point of view. Critical thinking has been associated with distinguishing facts from opinions when discovering a topic.

Critical Thinking For Students

These pieces of training have been designed to assist in critical thinking skills.

1. **Tour guide for Alien**

The exercise will give chance to reason beyond your normal way of thinking and seeing things. Take an example where you have been allocated the task of handling tour of aliens who are coming to the earth to study human life. You are in a blimp, having a view of the landscape and you fly over professional baseball stadium. As you pass over an alien gets curious and asks about what is happening and asks many questions like:

- What is a game?
- Why there are no ladies in the game?
- Why people are excited about watching others play?
- What is a team?

- Why people on the stands are not joining the ones playing?

You answer the questions fully then it can be fast to come up with certain assumptions and values. You can give an answer like "we support a particular team because they bring us together as a community." Having a community in your statement is a value that is considered by many people. When explaining team sports to an alien then make sure you give the value about winning and losing. Thinking like an alien tour guide will force you to look deeply at the things we do and value. At times they are not logical when you look at them from the outside.

2. Fact or Opinion

You have to be aware of the difference between fact and opinion, and it's not easy to distinguish. Anytime you visit a website how do feel about the things you read? Due to the availability of so much data, it's easy for students to enhance critical thinking skills. You have to be keen and use trustworthy sources for your school assignments and projects. You can be in a world full of assumptions as you already know when you aren't capable to distinguish between fact and opinion. In this exercise, you have to be very keen on what you are reading just to tell whether it's a fact or opinion. You can do this alone or by a study partner.

- I have the best mum in the world.
- My dad is shorter than your dad.
- Your phone number is a bit tricky to have in mind.
- Deepest part of the lake 15,789 feet deep.
- Dogs are man's best friend.
- Drinking too much is not good for your health.
- Most of the American citizens are color blind.
- Most of the cancer cases are brought about by smoking.

Critical Thinking in the Workplace

There are some ways that you can use to promote critical thinking in your workplace. The topics below are some of the ways to enhance critical thinking at your organization:

1. Hiring and promoting critical thinkers

The first and very important step to take in enhancing team spirit in critical thinking is to hire people who have gained experience in that area. Character interview is a better way of weighing your candidate's capability in critical assessment and inquiry. Making of critical thinking a desired competency for leadership and promotion then you will have started the journey of building a great growth of gifted critical thinkers.

2. Building A Learning Culture

You have to have an environment that occupies characters associated to critical thinking are a natural part of your industry values. There are some ways you can engage in building and supporting culture that stimulates critical analysis like:

- Incorporate the lessons learned discussions after the end of a project, where employees have the opportunity to see and apply on areas where critical thinking can be of help to enhance a project's production.
- Create an environment that has tough questions being asked and allow all your employees to be part of it to talk freely alternatively.
- Have a plan for decision making that gives positive energy to critical thinking such as having solutions to problems, exploring bias, and taking in charge the consequences of various suggested solutions.

3. Don't Jump Into Conclusions

To enhance critical thinking in your workplace then you ought not to jump into conclusions. Solve a problem by having a common understanding of the challenges it has. There are a few tips on how to achieve this:

- Find out the origin of a problem by asking questions.
- Describe the outcome before you are satisfied with settling on a resolution to the problem.
- Don't overthink on finding a solution, because it will slow down the process of solving the problem and limit disciplined thoughts.

4. Creating on internal forums

The act of talking things out can be a great step to help to solve a problem. Having a for where you can address and talk about your issues help in generating new ideas and helps in developing good working environs and creates resolutions to problems at your workplace.

5. Teaching And Training

Developing leadership and unity skills training can be of great positivity to help enhance the critical thinking strengths of your employees by creating a mindset and skillset change. People will get new characters and start to see the wider side of handling problems and how to solve them. Having experiential learning can be a positive step as it promotes critical thinking by learning and doing. This approach will fully engage employees, and they will continually enhance the critical and problem solving skills. The building of a rule that enhances and encourage critical thinking in your company will have you achieve great results and products.

Powerful Skills Related To Critical Thinking

There are various techniques that can be used in teaching critical thinking skills in each lesson and subject. You can research and have the ways and incorporate them in your day to day teaching practices:

1. **Start with a question**

Beginning with an open way to get into the subject. What you want to talk about and explore. The question should not be the one to be answered with a yes or no. for you to improve on questions then you have to inspire the urge for solving problems. It can give you the support of improving your critical things in the best way possible. Questions you are asking students should be giving room to them to brainstorm. You can note down answers on the chalkboard and open talks giving students an advantage of defining the problem and its solution.

2. **Creation of a foundation**

Students find it hard to think critically if the information they want is not there or they access it. Any exercise should start with reviewing related data that ensures you can think of the facts related to the topic. The items are:

- Read assignments and homework.
- Previous classes and tasks.
- Video or text.

3. **Consulting classics**

Classical literary works perfectly by launching pad for exploring great brain work. You can use them for detailed lessons to builder character motivation, predictions, and theme. There are some links that can help you to explore resources:

- Skeptic north
- Critical thinking community
- Shakespeare and critical thinking

4. **Creation of a country**

This can be a great project to study the situation of your country. Students can study history, geography, politics and many more. There are some resources that can help you:

- Geography site
- Can you start your own country?

- Ways to start your micro-nation

5. Using information eloquence

Students are supposed to be well informed to enhance their success in school and life. You have to learn how to access a lot of info and have appropriate ways of solving a problem. Students should be able to enhance their thinking capabilities. When you teach critical thinking skills it will be sustained by an understanding of information fluency.

6. Utilization of peer groups

When you have numbers, you will possibly have comfort. Digital kids living in environments that have teamwork and collaboration. You have to make kids realize there is excellent cause of info, questions, and problem-solving performances.

7. Try a sentence

You can try the exercise by having groups of 10 students. After which you instruct every student to note one sentence talking about the topic on a sheet of paper. After writing the student is supposed to pass the paper to the next single sentence. But as they pass the paper it is supposed to be folded to cover the sentence. With that, just one sentence will be seen and not any other and every time you pass it students will only see one sentence. This task will add more steps in their understanding. It teaches them to apply knowledge and logic to describe themselves clearly.

8. Problem solving

When you assign a certain problem it can be the best avenue for teaching critical thinking skills. You are supposed to leave the goal open-ended for a larger possible tactic. This is one reason why you should ask convenient questions that want discovery of knowledge through critical thinking. When you have the right process to see you through, then you will realize its best to teach critical thinking and problem solving skills.

9. Return to role-playing

Role of playing is considered to be a great method of practicing critical thinking. This is why most actors do a lot of research that involves inhabiting persona and its appearances. When you are taking someone's character, it helps in expanding your analytical and creative thinking skills. Put students together and let them research on a topic like conflict involving communication amid famous historical statistics. Have them decide which character they will play. Each one of them will have different views in regards to the conflict. Let them discuss the conflict until each one is able to talk about their views. A challenge that will be faced is when everyone is supposed to suggest a compromise.

Chapter 8: Critical Thinking Vs Non-Critical Thinking

What is Non-Critical Thinking?

Non-critical thinking is accepting as accurate, things that are not supported by any evidence. It is choosing what to do or say based only on emotion, or jumping to an answer or conclusion without working your way through the separate parts of the issue. It amounts to assumptive leaps of faith. If you are a non-critical thinker, then you most often defer your thinking to others and accept their conclusions wholeheartedly. Non-critical thinking occurs when you don't comment, challenge, or draw a comparison with other choices of the information you are presented with.

When Do Non-Critical Thinking Likely To Happen To You?

Non-critical thinking can occur if you are experiencing the following situations:

- In stressful situations that happen very fast and you end up reacting before you have had time to think things through. You act impulsively without thinking in such circumstances. You may end up saying things or engaging in actions which makes you feel quite uncomfortable much later when you have had time to critically assess the situation and weigh the other options you should have considered

- Another possibility revolves around human perception, and that is when a situation occurs, and you perceive the situation as familiar or normal and therefore assume that you can deal with the situation in the usual way only for you to discover much later that you misperceived the true nature of the situation

- Non-critical thinking can also occur when you extremely focus on a complicated task. You end up becoming immersed so much in the task that you forget the big picture and the reason for engaging in the task in the first place.
- Another situation that can trigger non-critical thinking is when you are involved in highly emotional situations with intense emotional consequences. Such situations occur when you face options, all of which are bad and which will result in severe loss.

Background of Critical Thinking

Critical thinking is comparatively a new way of thinking, teaching, and learning. But the roots of critical thinking are as ancient as the teaching practice and roots of Socrates 2500 years ago. Socrates discovered, by a method of probing questioning that people could not rationally justify their confident claims to knowledge. He demonstrated that a person may have power and position and yet be deeply confused and irrational. He established the importance of asking deep questions that probe profoundly, into thinking before you accept ideas as worthy to belief. His method of thinking is now known as 'Sarcastic Questioning'. It is the best-known critical thinking teaching strategy. In his mode of questioning, Socrates highlighted the need of thinking for clarity and logical consistency

Later Socrates' practice was followed by the critical thinking of Plato, Aristotle, and the Greek skeptics. They all emphasized that things are very different from what they appear to be and that only trained mind is prepared to see through the way things look to us on the surface to the way they really are beneath the surface

In the middle ages, the tradition of systematic critical thinking was embodied in the writings and teaching of such thinkers as Thomas Aquinas who heightened our awareness not only of the potential power of reasoning but also of the need for . to be systematically cultivated and cross-examined

In the Renaissances period between the 15th and 16th century, a group of scholars from Europe among them Francis Bacon began to think critically about religion, art, society, human nature, law, and freedom. Bacon recognized that the mind could not be left safely to its natural tendencies. His book 'The Advancement of Learning' is considered one of the earliest texts in critical thinking. Bacon developed a method of critical thought based on the principle of systematic thought. He argued that every part of thinking should be questioned, doubted and tested.

At the same time, Sir Thomas Moore developed a new system of social order called Utopia, in which every domain of the present world was subject to critique.

In the 19th century, critical thought was extended further into the areas of human social life by Comte and Spencer

The basics of critical thinking are that the fundamental questions of Socrates can now be much more powerfully framed and used. In every domain of human thought and within every use of reasoning within, it is now possible to question. In other words, questioning that focuses on these fundamentals of theory and logic are now baseline in critical thinking.

Differences between Critical Thinking and Ordinary Thinking

Ordinary thinking is intuitive thinking. You don't question your own decisions and opinions. Therefore, the views and decisions you make using ordinary thinking will be biased and lacks in objectivity.

On the other hand, critical thinking requires you to think about your actions and decisions actively. You look at life and its problems in a very objective way. If you perform critical thinking correctly, then the opinion you form will be free from bias. The decisions you make will also be very objective and logical.

Another difference between critical and ordinary thinking is speed. Ordinary thinking tends to be fast. Decisions are reached very fast, with a high possibility of making so many errors and being biased. On the other hand, critical thinking tends to be slow but with objective results which are free from any biasness.

Below is a comparative table that will further help you understand the differences between critical thinking and ordinary thinking;

Critical thinking	Ordinary thinking
Critical thinking involves practicing restrained and controlling your feelings rather than being controlled by them. It is also about thinking before you act.	Ordinary thinking is when you tend to follow your feelings and act impulsively.
Critical thinking requires you to avoid extreme views because they are seldom correct. You should also practice fair-mindedness and seek a balanced view.	In ordinary thinking, you ignore the need for balance and instead give preference to opinions that support your own established views.
In critical thinking, you need to be interested in other people's ideas. You are	In ordinary thinking, you are preoccupied with yourself and your own opinions, and

expected to read and listen attentively even when you tend to disagree with the views of the other person.	you fail to pay attention to the views of others.
Critical thinking expects you to set aside your personal preferences and base judgments on evidence. You are required to defer judgment in situations where evidence is lacking or is insufficient. You also revise your judgments when new evidence reveals error contradicting your earlier judgments.	Ordinary thinking base judgments on first impressions and gut reactions. You are not bothered to find out the amount of evidence to support your judgment. You also tend to cling on earlier views even in the face of new evidence more prior beliefs.
In critical thinking, you strive for understanding, keep curiosity alive, remain patient with complexity, and you are ready to invest time to overcome confusion in a given situation.	Ordinary thinking, you are impatient with complexity, and you prefer remaining confused than make an effort to understand a situation.
In critical thinking problems and challenging issues are opportunities for you to learn.	Ordinary thinking regards issues as nuisance or threats to your ego.
In critical thinking, you are honest to yourself. You also acknowledge what you don't know. You tend to recognize your limitations, and you monitor your errors.	In ordinary thinking, you pretend you know more than you do. You also tend to ignore your weaknesses and assume your views are error-free.

Characteristics of Critical Thinkers

Curiosity

Critical thinkers possess an insatiable level of curiosity. They are curious about a wide range of issues that interest them. They have a healthy inquisitiveness about the people and the world. Critical thinkers tend to be interested in understanding and appreciation for the diversity of beliefs, cultures, and views that encompasses humanity. They are lifelong learners willing to learn through daily situations and experiences they go through.

Compassion

Critical thinkers act as much with their hearts as with their minds. They recognize that each person has a story of their life that makes them who they are. They also appreciate the fact that individuals have personal trials and challenges that shape them. They then passionately celebrate the uniqueness in everyone and are willing to help you see the best in yourselves and the others. They embrace the emotional instinctual as much as the intellectuals of others

Awareness

Critical thinkers are always aware of opportunities around them which requires the application of critical thinking skills. They are still alert for the opportunities to apply their best thinking habits to any situation presented to them. They have a desire to think critically about even the simplest of issues and tasks with a thirst for constructive outcomes.

Critical thinkers don't take things at face value. They keep asking questions and explore all sides of an issue. They look for the more profound facts hiding within all modes of data. This way, those who think critically tend to be the best problem solvers

Decisiveness

Situations involving critical thinking often requires you to make a quick and decisive action. When you think critically, you tend to weigh your options and look at the possible outcomes of a situation. You, therefore, need speed and clarity, and you should be able to put aside any fear when it comes to decision making. An excellent critical thinker strives to move things forward fast instead of procrastinating.

Sometimes you have to make quick choices even when you don't have all the necessary information about a specific situation. You, therefore, need to make such choices in confidence. You should be able to take the lead and make hard decisions which others are afraid of whenever you are facing any challenge. If you are an effective critical thinker, then you should realize the necessity of taking the initiative and make quick decisions even if it ends up being the wrong one, because any choice is better than none.

Honesty

Honesty is an essential virtue to a critical thinker. Moral integrity, ethical consideration, and action are imperative hallmarks of capable critical thinkers. Honest people have a desire for harmony and fulfillment.

The practice of honesty in critical thinking also extends to how you look within yourself to embrace what reside sleep inside your soul. Honesty takes into account the process determining how you manage your emotions, how you control your impulses and recognizing any attempts at self-deception. Critical thinkers also accept themselves and the others for who they are.

Creativity

Effective critical thinkers are outstanding creative thinkers. Practical critical thinking in business, marketing, and any other profession relies heavily on your ability to be creative. When you get creative at how you package and market your product or service, you will expect handsome rewards in the global market place.

Critical thinkers tend to perceive the world in new ways to find hidden patterns and to make connections between what seems to be an unrelated phenomenon and to generate solutions.

Willingness

Willingness and flexibility are some of the critical considerations of critical thinkers. Willingness includes the following abilities:

- Ability to learn from your own mistakes and shortcomings to be a better critical thinker
- You strive to improve, learn and excel continually in what you do
- You don't fear to challenge the status quo whenever you are faced with situations which demand you do so
- You tend to be open-minded and take considerations of other people's opinions which may challenge yours
- Whenever you are presented with new evidence, you are willing to reconsider your past views
- You listen attentively and actively at all times rather than just waiting for your turn to talk

Objectivity

Good critical thinkers are very objective in their thinking and reasoning. They focus on facts and scientific evaluation of the information at hand. They tend to keep their emotions and those from others from affecting their judgment. Critical thinkers are aware of their biases, and they tend to look at issues dispassionately.

Eating Habits that Boost your Critical Thinking

Taking Coffee in Moderate Levels
Coffee contains caffeine. Coffee is the most consumed stimulant in the world. It has been referenced to have on attention and mental alertness. Many studies have shown that caffeine ingestion leads to increased stimulation of your heart. The studies have also demonstrated that caffeine leads to enhanced cognitive performance involving various tasks. It has a positive effect on vigilance, mental alertness and multiple domains of attention.

Caffeine also reduces response times and error rates. Your brain loves caffeine too. Brain processes which respond well to caffeine include selective visual attention, task switching, response inhibition, and conflict monitoring.

However, you should note that higher doses of coffee can have adverse effects on your health. Too many doses of coffee can also negatively affect your thinking ability and also can cause anxiety, confused thoughts, and speech. It is recommended that you take one or two cups of coffee in the morning after eating something first.

Ingest Low Sugar Levels
You may be tempted to eat sugary snacks or processed food to raise your blood sugars when it dips. However, doing so may only serve to increase your blood sugars and energy levels for a short period after which you go through a slump. This is because sugar is digested and used very fast and cannot sustain the energy needed for thinking. You will then end up lacking focus, and your reaction time will be delayed.

Studies have shown that eating sugar can have an adverse biological impact on your mind and brain. The studies drew a strong connection between sugar intake and diminishment of how you well remember instructions and process ideas.

It is recommended that instead of taking sugar, you should take more high protein and high fiber foods to give you focus throughout the day and curb sugar cravings. If you are craving something sweet, you can go for healthy fruits like the apple. You can also eat some raw veggie sticks before dinner to add more fiber to your diet.

Eat more nuts

Studies have shown that eating nuts could significantly improve your brain function linked to cognition, healing, learning, and memory. Nuts like pistachios are best for improving cognition processing and learning. It also helps your brain to retain information for more extended periods. Walnuts have also been shown to increase your reasoning skills which are vital for critical thinking. Nuts are right for your brain as they are also good for the rest of the body.

Don't overdo it

Sometimes you engage in too much activity which could have adverse effects on your general wellbeing Between deadlines, play, exercise, work and everything in between, your body and mind can act as an indicator to alert you on when you are pushing too far. If you are often feeling tired, it could be a sign that your body is burned out and you need rest. To be an excellent critical thinker, you should avoid too much exercise, alcohol, smoking, or eating too much or too little.

Obstacles of Critical Thinking and How to Overcome Them

Lack of clear direction and plan
One of the biggest obstacles to critical thinking is a lack of clear goals and objectives on your part. Sometimes you may come up with goals, but they are not detailed, and they may lack a clear plan on how to implement them.

You should be clear of what you want to achieve and state the time limit as well as your action plan. This way, your mind becomes organized, and you focus better on achieving your set goals.

Being afraid of failure
When you fear to fail, then your mind is automatically hindered from thinking critically. The fear of failure or loss or making a mistake may prevent you from making that right decision that could change your life.

It is the possibility of failure and the expectation of failure that paralyzes action and becomes the key reason for failure and ineffective problem solving.

Fear of rejection
You may postpone making a decision simply because you fear how other people close to you may react over it. You fear facing rejection or being mocked for your choice. You fear you may sound dumb and foolish before your family and friends. You end up living a life of underachievement because you are afraid to sell yourself or your ideas for success.

The tendency to retain the status quo
Critical thinking is hampered by your desire to maintain a stable and constant environment. You tend to suffer from a

subconscious desire to remain consistent with what you have done or said in the past. You tend to be afraid of saying or doing something new which is different from what you said or did in the past.

This tendency, unfortunately, leads you to your comfort zone, which, in the end, hampers your progress.

Failure to think proactively

If you fail to stimulate your mind with new knowledge and ideas continually, it loses its vitality and energy, and your thinking tends to be passive and automatic. If you want to avoid passivity, then you should consider altering your routine to challenge your mind. Change the time you wake up and get out and meet new friends once in a while. Find out new ideas of doing things for your mind to be kept engaged.

You rationalize and fail to improve

Rationalizing is an attempt to explain or justify behaviors or attitudes with logical reasons, even if these are inappropriate. It is a defense mechanism on your part in which you try to justify controversial behavior or feelings, and you explain it in a seemingly rational and logical manner to avoid the correct explanation. Rationalization encourages irrational or unacceptable behavior, motives, and feeling. Rationalization, therefore, goes against the best practices of a capable critical thinker.

Critical Habits of the Mind

Truth-seeking

You always look for intellectual integrity and a desire to actively strive for the best possible knowledge in any given situation. You tend to ask probing questions and follow reasons and evidence wherever they lead you to.

Open-minded

you practice open-mindedness by being tolerant of other persons divergent views, and you are open to the possibility of their own biasness.

Analytical

You tend to be alert on potential problems, and you look out for the possible consequences of the issues at hand. You also foresee long term and shorter outcomes of events, actions, and decisions.

Inquisitive mind

You tend to aim at being well informed at all times. You are curious to know how things work and seek to learn new things about a wide range of topics. You possess a strong sense of intellectual curiosity.

Systematic

You tend to take an organized and thorough approach to identify and resolve problems. You tend to be orderly, persistent, focused, and diligent in your approach to problem-solving, learning and inquiry.

Chapter 9: Problem-Solving—Steps, Process, and Techniques

Problem solving is the way you attain a goal from a present state, wherein the present state, you either don't directly move toward the goal, you're far from it, or you need more complex logic to find steps towards the goal. When it comes to solving problems, you have to work through every aspect of an issue then find the best solution to solve it. You often fear or at times get uncomfortable when problems arise. It's a problem itself to be faced with a problem that's why each problem needs a solution. The biggest mistake in solving a problem is trying to find a solution immediately. That's a mistake because what you need is a solution at the end. Finding solutions immediately puts the solution at the beginning of the process, which messes up with the whole thing. You solve a problem when you reach a goal or state.

The more difficult and important the problem, the more helpful and necessary it is to use a disciplined process. Unique knowledge bases are used to approach various problems situations. The bases are basic expectations of how the universe works. When you identify, interpret and evaluate a problem, it's mostly based on what you already know. For example, a hotel manager might know why a certain problem is more important and urgent than the other because it is only him or her who has full knowledge of their department. Knowledge might, therefore, help or hinder problem solving.

In this chapter, we are going to understand the definition of a problem, the analysis, and synthesis of a problem as well as describe the process of problem solving.

Definition Of A Problem

A problem is a situation or matter that is seen as harmful and needs to be overcome. A problem can also be referred to as the factor that is unsatisfactory and causes difficulties in the day-to-day living of people. The word problem, however, has diverse meanings ranging from business problems to organization problems. The problem can be best understood and made familiar with the use of other words like difficulty.

Problem Analysis

Problem analysis is the research done on a problem to find out its cause to identify an improvement on a system, procedure, process, design, or culture. Problem analysis is majorly focused on finding the root cause and effect of a given problem and establishes ways of resolving the issue. The key to problem analysis is defining the problem, having evidence of the problem, imparts of the problem, finding the causes, and establishing the recommendations of the existing problem. The suggestions are, in most cases, the reverse of the purposes of the issues.

This problem solving process is essential in the sense that it can be used to analyze a problem, understand it, and generate a range of improvement opportunities. It also is useful in assessing opportunities and determining the probable benefits in the event of seizing them. There exist four types of problem analysis;

> **Cause and effect analysis** – This method of problem analysis deals with finding out the causes and the effects brought about by a problem.
> **Root cause analysis** – This analysis method singles out the leading cause of a problem from all the probable causes of a problematic situation.

The five whys- Asking of five why questions in a consecutive manner help to realize and reveal the deeper causes of a given problem.

The fishbone diagram- This is a method of viewing the problem from different angles basing on the multiple root cases found out. The technique can be used to suggest recommendations on fixing the issues.

There are steps towards problem analysis, and they have been proved to help in solving and reduce the effects of problems. The steps work differently depending on the situation and the characters involved. Schools, workplaces, churches all have each their problem analysis procedures that best suits them. The one discussed below is those applying to a majority of individuals.

1. Understand the problem

The first step towards self-help and meditation, an individual needs to understand the symptoms and nature of what he is experiencing. This involves identifying the quality of the problem and why and how it became to be a challenge for you. It is advised we own up for any responsibility or faults that might have led to the difficulty being experienced rather than inappropriately blame others. If possible, one needs to talk out the situation to a trusted friend to gain and find out their perspective on the issue, this way understanding the situation better hence easy to know how to go about reversing it.

2. Break the problem into smaller parts

The problem may be too big or is a tangle-web of many challenges together. Solving or looking for solutions in that form may prove tiresome and not easily manageable to fix it all at once. The problem needs to be broken down into small manageable parts, and a plan set up for solving them one after the other separately. Identifying the first problem that led to all the others is key to breaking down the problem. This knowledge aids in illuminating the next issue and steps that should be taken in solving them.

3. Define your problem goals

Small manageable problems at one point need to be eliminated. There should be goals towards this to complete the self-help process for each part of the bigger problem. If one doesn't have goals or strategies, then it will be a hard task to notice if the problem has been ended or its effects are still faced. The goals are defined upon having a clear understanding of the problematic situation and root causes identified. The objectives, therefore, are the methods describing how and when is the reversing the purposes of the problem done and the result expected after that.

4. Decide on how to measure progress towards problem goals

Goals may be lined up to curb a situation depending on the specific problem. The best goal suiting the issue is decided on following factors that favor those affected by the problem. The factors include; what the problem's starting point is, how far has one gone towards achieving the goal and how will one know he's met the target and is done with the problem.

Synthesis Of A Problem

While problem analysis involves breaking down a problem into different components, the combination of a problem combines many ideas into a single one to understand the shared quality of the plans. Synthesis of a problem is considered to be more future-oriented as it perceives the 'what could be' statement rather than 'what can I do' comment. It is focused more on understanding the problem as well as establishing the potential solutions from the future from a combination of perception, knowledge, and imagination. It offers a comprehensive and elaborate way of solving issues since it involves strategic thinking and the synthesis skill of envisioning the larger picture on an issue. Synthesis of a problem provides critical aspects effortlessly towards solving both existing problems and new problems.

Problem synthesis bases more on the long-term approach to solving problems. This is because solving a problem includes not only seeing the actual problem but also finding a solution to the problem. Rushing through the whole process could lead to perhaps causing more problems. Synthesis puts together the art of 'it is possible' and makes a combination of different elements looking into the context in which the problem was caused and happened and then expanding on it in all areas possible making it a whole more significant problem. Many leaders lack a synthesizing lens in their problem-solving duties. This leads to more questions instead of problem-solving in the end due to not understanding the issue critically. Therefore, they should equip themselves with self-aware and offer professional maturity in the role they play in solving problems.

The synthesizing mind tends to look at complex problems as a whole instead of dividing into small manageable pieces. When it comes to solving problems, it is advisable to leverage systems for problem framing since problem framing helps one to take on a broad open perspective and solve the problem without creating too many other new issues. System lens also helps one to see a more comprehensive system with interactive pieces and conflict resolution goals.

Importance of Problem Solving

We all play a role in problem-creating or solving through our words, actions, and even thoughts. Problem solving is the ability to reverse the adverse effects of a problem in an effective way. Problem solving involves defining the problem, generating alternatives to the problem, and choosing the best option to implement. Question-solving skill and technique are equally important to both individuals and organizations because it enhances exerting of control and authority in the environment. The importance of solving problems within the community include the discussed below;

1. Fixing broken things

Step employed towards solving a problem contributes to the overall effectiveness and change in a challenge. Questions reflect on broken relationships, procedures, and hence a mechanism for identifying these and deduce measures and methods of fixing them. Reasons for the breakage determining a course of action is all part of solving the problem.

2. Addressing risks

Intelligence has enabled people to fix problems as they arise as well as have skills to anticipate future happenings based on past experiences and trends. Problem-solving art is also applicable to such and also can be used to enable immediate actions to influence the possibility of even occurring again as before or alter its impact. Researchers have managed to develop and learn trends of cause and effect on the relationship of problems and their origins in different environments and times.

3. Improving performance

Individuals and organizations cannot exist solely without depending on one another and having relationship ties. The action of one, therefore, affects the other person or an organization either directly or indirectly. The act of interdependence among individuals and organization to organization enhances teamwork and creates a force of unity towards solving more complex problems. Problem-solving helps us to have a deeper understanding of relations and implement changes and improvements needed to compete earnestly and survive in a dynamic environment.

4. Seeking opportunity

Solving is also about creating new things and innovations towards achieving a more desirable environment. It allows us to come through different opportunities, which we can exploit and exert control over.

5. To make decisions

Is essential to learn the skills of problem-solving since we all have to make decisions a few times in our lives, whether a student or parent. This is because each person faces problems every day at their levels. Issue solving skill is critical and essential that all persons develop and refine them through training, practice, or learning from others.

The Problem Solving Process

The problem solving process consists of the following steps:

Problem identification

The problem at hand must be clear. You must identify the right source of a problem to not make the steps carried out be rendered useless. Assumptions must not be made in order to solve the problem at hand. For example, if you have a problem with work performance. First, you have to identify the cause of the problem.it can be as a result of inadequate sleep or too much workload. But if you assume the problem is work being too difficult then the problem won't be solved.

Problem to be interpreted

The problem must be well interpreted and understood once it has been identified. The best solution is the one that ensures everyone's issue is addressed. In order to get solutions with different perspectives, those different perspectives to understand any problem must be considered. For example, after identifying that the problem is too much workload affecting your work performance, you need to interpret and understand the problem itself and its cause after that you then sort out reasons behind the problem.

Strategy formation

A strategy must be well developed to help you find the best solution. You must formulate different strategies for every different situation; it must also depend on the unique preference of each individual. Let's take the example of the problem with work performance. After identifying and understanding the problem, a strategy must be drawn. Try to formulate a work plan to manage the workload at the same time be able to have enough sleep which will, in turn, lead to better work performance.

Information to be organized

There must be a revision of strategies and refinement for perfect results. The solutions accuracy greatly depends on the information amount provided. What is known and not known about the problem at hand must be considered to help find out more about the problem.

Resources to be allocated

Because resources like money, time and the latter are very limited, you must decide how high the priority is to solve your problem which will, in turn, help you identify the ones you'll be using to find the solution. If the problem is important, you can allocate more resources to solving it. However, if the problem is not as important, it's not worth the time and money. Let's take an example where you land a job in a different country. The problem here is if there are enough resources available to solve the issue of expenses and whether or not you'll get your money back after travelling all the way. If there is the profit earned then why not.

Progress to be monitored

For you to be effective in solving problems you must regularly monitor your progress. Each progress must be well documented. And, if you're not making as much progress as they're supposed to, you have to reevaluate the approach taken or either way to look for new strategies. Let's take the first example where the problem was work performance. After all the right steps are taken for the problem, progress must as well be monitored for perfect results to be attained.

Results to be well evaluated

Lastly, you need to evaluate the solution to find out if it's the best possible solution to the problem at hand. Even though a solution has been found it does not end at that. The evaluation might either be immediate or it might take a while. Let's take an example of an answer to a science problem can be checked then and there, however a solution to your yearly issue with returns in taxes might be impossible to be evaluated right there.

Techniques and tools needed for Problem Solving

In order to effectively solve a problem, it is crucial that we use important techniques which are useful;

Create a team (teamwork): you will be able to effectively discuss the problem at hand because as it is well known two heads are better than one. Teamwork also leads to creativity and assist in thinking out of the box.

Have a fishbone diagram: Also known as the cause and effect diagram(C&E), this helps you explore all the potential and real causes that normally lead to a single failure or defect. It is used for brainstorming purposes. The brainstorming session can effectively act like a great method of obtaining ideas and causes. For example, all participants can present their ideas, and the one collecting ideas can record them. Unusual ideas are welcome, and it is important to focus on quantity.

Use the five why's to help get to the actionable root cause of the problem. It is important to base your whys on facts and observations, not opinions. For example, when the problem at hand is why your car won't start then the whys can be; why? – The battery is dead; why? - The alternator is not working; why? - The alternator belt has broken; why? - The alternator belt has never been replaced; why? - You have not been well maintained the car. The last why should always be the root cause of the problem. You should be able to make the tools work for you and not be a slave to the tools.

Barriers of Problem Solving

Effective problem solving takes more attention, time and willingness to slow down. But less time and attention than is required by a problem not well solved. It is not always a strictly linear exercise working through this process. With these, we have various barriers:

Information irrelevance. This is when unrelated information that won't help solve a problem is presented as part of it. Typically, it detracts from the process of problem-solving, because it may seem pertinent and at the same time distract you from finding the most efficient solution. An example of a problem hindered by irrelevant information is. The answer, of course, is none of them: if they are in the phone book, they do not have unlisted numbers. But the extraneous information at the beginning of the problem makes many people believe they have to perform a mathematical calculation of some sort. This is the trouble that irrelevant information can cause.

Functional fixedness and mental set. Functional fixedness occurs when the intended purpose of an object hinders a person's ability to see its potential other uses. For example, say you need to open a lid in a metal container, but you only have a hammer. You might not realize that you could use the pointy, two-pronged end of the hammer to puncture the top of the tin since you are so accustomed to using the hammer as simply a pounding tool a mental set is an unconscious tendency to approach a problem in a particular way. Our mental sets are shaped by our past experiences and habits. For example, if the last time your phone froze you restarted it and it worked, that might be the only solution you can think of the next time it freezes.

Constraints being unnecessary. This barrier shows up in problem-solving causing people to unconsciously place boundaries on the task at hand. A famous example of this barrier to problem solving is the dot problem. In this problem, there are nine dots arranged in one square. The one solving the problem is asked to draw not more than four lines, without lifting their pen or pencil from the paper that connects all of the dots. What often happens is that the solver creates an assumption in their mind that they must connect the dots without letting the lines go outside the square of dots. The solvers are literally unable to think outside the box. Standardized procedures of this nature often involve mentally invented constraints of this kind.

It is true that the major fault of problem-solving is jumping to conclusions. You can also say that object problems are easier to solve than people problems because the people who anticipate potential problems are generally thought to be negative.

Chapter 10: Problem Solving Skills

Problem solving has slightly different meanings depending on the discipline in question. In psychology, it is a mental process while in computer science it is a computerized process. Whatever the discipline or situation, whether at school or at work, whether within the family or in a public gathering, you will be faced with a problem. You will be required to come up with a solution to the problem you are facing as soon as possible to avoid a standstill.

You will require a special set of skills commonly referred to as problem solving skills. So what exactly are these skills that you are always hearing about? How do you acquire them and most importantly, when and how do you apply these said skills? Problem solving skills are traits that enable you to assess the situation and calmly come up with a solution. They help you determine the source of the standoff without being prejudice critically think about the problem then offer a lasting solution that is favorable to both parties.

These skills are acquired over time with years of experience. They are important in every career at any level and as a result effective problem solving may require job-specific technical skills. While problem solving skills are required by employers, they are also highly useful in other aspects of life like interpersonal relationships and day to day decision making.

A lot of the work in problem solving involves understanding what the underlying issues of the problem really are and not just what can be seen. For example, when dealing with a complaint from the customer, it may seem wise to deal with the problem as soon as possible. It is actually right to quickly find a solution to the problem to avoid angering the customer and losing customers as a consequence. However, the employee dealing with the complaint should be asking themselves what actually caused the problem in the first place. This way, recurrence of the problem can be avoided in future.

Although problem solving skills are often described as its own separate skill, there are other related skills that contribute to this acquired ability. Below we discuss some of the key problem solving skills:-

Active listening

Listening is the most important component of interpersonal communication skills. It is not something that just happens; instead, it is an active process in which one chooses to listen and understand the messages of the speaker. As a skill, it can be acquired and developed over time with continued practice. It involves fully concentrating on the message of the speaker rather than just passively hearing what the speaker has to say.

When solving a problem, you will have to be a great listener. You will have to listen to both parties that are involved in the standoff and actually understand what it is they are trying to say. Signs of active listening include but are not limited to smiling, maintaining eye contact, appropriate posture and ability to mirror the speaker's facial expressions. It also involves asking questions where one cannot understand.

When you actually listen and understand both parties, it becomes possible for you to come up with a lasting solution that does not favor either of the parties.

Research

This is an essential skill in solving a problem, be it in a simple or complex situation. As a problem solver you will be required to identify the cause of the problem and understand it fully. This could involve a simple Google search in simple situations or a more rigorous research project in complex situations such as when writing a research thesis.

You begin by gathering more information concerning the situation by listening to testimonials from fellow team members and employees. Then you will be required to verify the information gathered by either enquiring from a second party or by use of hard evidence as in books or digital devices. You can then consult more experienced employees on a way forward concerning the issue or do online research before arriving at your solution.

This way you will be able to offer a solution to a problem that you not only understand its root cause but also the chronology of events leading to the standoff.

Analytical thinking

Analytical thinking is the detailed examination of elements or structure of something. This results in additional knowledge, solutions or ideas related to the problem or topic. It is a complex process that involves identifying a problem, gathering more information concerning the problem and developing solutions to your problem. Then you go ahead and test your new solution or idea based on the information you gathered before reviewing the situation to find out whether the solution worked or on.

Analytical skills are in demand in many industries and are commonly listed in the job requirements during a job advertisement.

Communication

Communication skill is perhaps one of the most important of all life skills as it important for not only maintaining work relations but also interpersonal relationships. Simply put communication is the act of transferring information from one place to another whether verbally, written or digitally. It enables us to pass information to other people and to understand and put into perspective what is being said to us.

When solving a problem, communication skills come in handy. Be it when trying to gather information around the problem or when passing information to the concerned parties on how to go about the situation. Appropriate verbal and body language needs to be used to avoid passing on the wrong message and hence creating more conflict than there already is.

Creativity

Problem solving and creativity go hand in hand. A lot of time can be wasted while trying to find a solution to a problem in the company. It is therefore important that you as the one in charge be rather creative to aid in time management. Come up with strategies that help in preventing the problem instead of waiting for it to happen so you can tackle it. You also need to be able to identify a problem in its early stages and come up with ways to prevent it from growing bigger and out of hand.

In short, as a savvy leader, it is entirely your responsibility to understand that the best approach to problem solving is to avoid a problem in the first place. Though it is technically impossible to avoid problems altogether, serious and time-wasting problems can be kept at bay using this approach. It involves creating an environment where employees are encouraged to use their initiative to remedy problems as soon as they occur. Furthermore, the manager and his employees should be able to sense problems before they occur. Also, problems should be seen as opportunities to learn and grown instead of as an obstacle.

Dependability

Dependability is a very important skill in problem solving. It is being capable of being depended on, of being worthy of trust. It is being responsible for your actions and not having the habit of putting the blame on others. It is finishing the assigned task on time. Not just finishing the task, but also doing your work thoroughly and submitting it within the time frame given. It is about being reliable that someone can depend on you and not wait to be disappointed.

Problems need to be identified and solved in a timely manner. As a problem solver, your fellow employees should be able to trust that you will be very reliable when handling the situation. They should trust that you will put the current situation first and that you will quickly and effectively carry out your investigations regarding the current situation. They should also believe you will not forget about what you were supposed to do leaving them without a solution to their problem. Problem solving is about taking charge of the situation like the leader you are and delivering the results in a timely and effective manner.

Decision making

Problem solving and decision making are two closely related skills. Decision making involves finally choosing one of the many solutions that you have in line. Not just coming to a conclusion but also choosing the most suitable and reliable solution. One that will favor both parties without being prejudice. It is about critically analyzing the situation and doing extensive research concerning the problem.

It is about accepting that you cannot only rely on your own intelligence to help solve the situation, that you need help either from more experienced staff or from print and digital media. It is about listing down all the solutions that you come up with and critically thinking and analyzing the situation to be able to choose one. The one solution chosen should be the most effective and suitable as per the situation. As the leader, it is therefore paramount that you be a good decision-maker. Your employees will be looking up to you to see what you will come with. It is your decision that will determine how the situation progresses. Whether it gets worse or you finally save the situation.

Team building

A team is a group of people who are brought together for a common purpose. Be it work or a committee for after activities such as a wedding or sports. All in all a team has a common goal and purpose. At your workplace, you are a team. Though in different departments, with probably different set goals, you all have one purpose as per the mission and vision of the company. Whether solving a problem at home, at work or when working on your thesis as a graduate student, teamwork is very crucial to the process of arriving at the solution.

It is therefore important that when solving a problem, each and every concerned party is involved in the process. Sensitive your subordinates and fellow employees on problem solving skills. Let them in on what is actually happening. Sensitive them on deadlines, difficulties with supplies or delays in making payments. Listen to your staff and make it clear that you are interested to hear what they have to say. When a problem arises, listen to both parties attentively and let them tell you how they feel concerning the situation. Let them tell you how they feel you should proceed.

Even in the face of trouble, let them feel like a team and work like one despite the challenges they are facing. When writing your thesis, the involvement of all stakeholders including your professor and your department is crucial. You will need them all at different times during the writing of your thesis.

Emotional intelligence

Emotional intelligence refers to the ability to identify and manage one's own emotions as well as the emotions of others. It is a crucial skill that is not only important in solving a problem but also when interacting with others. It enables you not to take things personally, to think maturely without only considering your emotions but most importantly those of others. It allows you to look at the problem critically and consider its emotional impact on the lives of those affected. To empathize with others and to put your own feelings aside.

This way, you will make a solution that considers the emotions of those affected. You will not go ahead and be heartless just because you feel the situation affects you more. Instead, the solution you make will be made from a sane point of view that is mature and free of the influence of one's emotions.

Risk management

Every action you take in your everyday life is a risk. When you decide to eat out instead of cooking, you are taking a risk as you do not know whether the food you are ordering is contaminated and would cause food poisoning. Even cooking for yourself is taking a risk as you do not know whether that is the day the gas decides to be faulty blowing up your house. With this in mind, it is important you note that problem solving involves taking a risk.

Even with adequate active listening, extensive research and consultation, the solution you arrive at carries a risk. You don't know whether it will be effective or it will end up creating more problems for you. Furthermore, you are not sure whether the rest of the staff will accept your solution. You will need to be agile to identify when your solution is working not working so you can quickly come up with another solution so as to quickly save the situation.

Below are a few tips on how to improve your problem solving skills

Acquire more technical knowledge in your field

Depending on the field you have specialized in, be it engineering, psychology or health sciences, it will be easier for you to solve problems in the field if you have adequate working technical knowledge. This way, you will not just be making decisions blindly or advising others by use of rumors you have heard. You gain more technical knowledge by doing back to school for additional course work, more training, and practice in your field of specialty.

Seek out opportunities to solve problems

Always put yourself in new situations. This could be you volunteering for new projects in your current role, on another team or outside your workplace for another organization. It is this way that you are likely to expose yourself to new opportunities to solve problems. You will slowly but surely gain the skills required to solve problems as you will be constantly faced with new challenges that the situation requires you to tackle.

Practice problems

As they say, practice makes better. Find appropriate practice tools for yourself. It could be practice books or online tutorials on how to solve problems. Choose the most appropriate one depending on your industry. These will expose you to different challenges that you would expect at your place of work. By trying to handle them at that time though theoretically, can help you quickly come up with effective solutions once faced with the same challenge at work.

Observe how others problem solve

At your place of work, there are definitely persons who are more experienced than you are no matter your position or rank. Just as children learn by observing and imitating what their elders are doing, so can we also learn. When a problem arises, and you are not the one solving it, it is important that you pay close attention as to what is happening. Closely follow the happenings of the problem and note down how the other person is handling the situation. This way, when faced with a similar situation, you will be able to tackle it with utmost confidence.

Every day of our lives, we are faced with a difficult situation, whether at school, work or home. These situations require us to look at things from all angles so we can come up with a suitable solution. It is therefore important that we train ourselves on how to handle such situations by first enlightening ourselves on suitable problem solving skills and then putting into practice what we have learnt. Let's not forget that these skills are applicable in all aspects of our lives, not just when job seeking. It is thus important that we acquire them for the sake of peaceful co-existence with others.

Conclusion

Thank you for making it through to the end of *BEGINNERS GUIDE TO CRITICAL THINKING AND PROBLEM SOLVING: Become a Better Critical Thinker & Problem Solver, by Using Secret Tools & Techniques That Will Boost These Skills & Your Decision Making Now!* Let us hope that the information was able to provide you with all the tools you need to become a better critical thinker and an effective problem solver. By finishing this book, you will be able to possess the mastery that you seek in making correct judgements of arguments and clearly analyzing and solving situations.

We have gone through the definition of critical thinking, the different types of critical thinking, the critical thinking framework, and the elements of intellectual standards. This book has offered easy-to-use but very powerful and effective techniques that students and the rest of the world can adopt to become better critical thinkers. You are now familiar with the reasons for embracing critical thinking and how to apply it in real life. You have also learned that you have the power to solve every problem, as long as you are willing to think in a critical, diverse manner.

For you to improve your critical thinking skills, it is vital that you encompass all the advice and techniques you have read herein. It may not be in the order that I listed them in this book, but you must use most of them for maximum benefits. You are now aware that become a great thinker and being able to reason well requires practice. The next thing you would want to do is to implement the things you have read here; this way, you will actualize the knowledge you have gained.

Finally, if you found this book useful in any way, an honest review is always appreciated!